History and Industrial Civilization

History and Industrial Civilization

R A BUCHANAN

St. Martin's Press   New York

All rights reserved. For information, write:
St. Martin's Press, Inc.
175 Fifth Avenue, New York, N.Y. 10010
Printed in Great Britain
First published in the United States of America in 1979

ISBN 0–312–37401–1

Library of Congress Cataloging in Publication Data

Buchanan, Robert Angus.
    History and industrial civilization.

    Includes bibliographical references and index.
1. Technology and civilization.   2. Europe—Civilization.
3. Civilization, Occidental.   I. Title.
CB478.B79   1979   909′.09′821   79–14550
ISBN 0–312–37401–1   FE 1 2'82 .

Contents

Iron sharpeneth iron; so a man sharpeneth the countenance of his friend.
PROVERBS 27 v.17.

Brian Geeson, Peter Olley, Bernard Israel, David Warren, Ian Livingstone, Glen Fallows, Sam Taylor, Maurice Marks, Peter Craddock, Jack Cheesman, David Johnson, T S Hamilton, A L Jones, F R Campbell, Ernst Hardy, Eric Waite, John Thomson, Christopher Hughes Smith, Mabel Mitchell, Charlie Woods, Neville Nicholson, Roy Pass, Tony Church, Bill Coates, John Punter, Mike Brookbank, Eddie Wignall, Gerald Manners, Margaret Davies, Hazel Holland, Peter Watkins, Peter Hall, John Vaizey, Tony Cross, Geoff Stokell, Oliver MacDonagh, Dick Gooderson, E E Rich, Alan Wilkinson, Garry Runciman, J J Knonshiel, John Herklotts, Richard Acland, Stanley Booth-Clibborn, Ted Wickham, Alan Ecclestone, George Macleod, Donald Soper, John Groser, Ethel Upton, H L Beales, Bill Hamling, Edwin Barker, Frank de Jonge, Alfred Jowett, Theo Barker, O R MacGregor, John Wayland, Johnny Cavanagh, Eric Moonman, Gerald Walters, Edward Horesh, Martin Swainston, Tony Benn, John Ollis, Julie Ollis, Mark Smith, Rita Hinden, Betty Vernon, Margaret Cole, John Lamble, John Cooper, George Wilkinson, John Totterdill, Ken Williams, Jane Williams, Adrian Wright, Mel Kranzberg, Gene Ferguson, Brooke Hindle, Jan DeArmond, Neil Cossons, Arthur Elton, Tom Rolt, George Watkins, John Butt, Michael Drake, Harry Armytage, John Harris, Keith Falconer, Rex Wailes, Rupert Hall, Margaret Weston, Paul Wilson, Brenda Buchanan.

Preface

History, on any definition, is about the past, and to many people the past is dead and irrelevant to the concerns of the present and the future. It is the purpose of this book to demonstrate that, far from being dead and irrelevant, the past contains all the most valuable experience we can acquire to help us to understand contemporary problems, and that the acquisition and application of such experience is a valid and, indeed, an indispensable exercise. It is the exercise of Applied History, and this book is concerned with exploring the possibilities of using knowledge of the past in achieving an understanding of the complex Industrial Civilisation of which we are all members.

The plan of the book is quite simple. It consists of a conceptual and analytical discussion of some of the major themes in the emergence of modern Industrial Civilisation, placed in the context of a chronological treatment of this development from the earliest civilised societies to the present day. Then, in the last two chapters, an attempt is made to assess the lessons of history and to outline projections derived from the study of history which indicate possible and even probable evolutionary patterns in the immediate and more remote future. The treatment is discursive rather than exhaustive: macro-historical rather than a succession of detailed micro-studies. The distinctive quality of this approach is its concentration on the single integrating objective of achieving an understanding of the dominant characteristics of our civilisation.

It would be unreasonable to expect the reader to agree with every aspect of the interpretation presented in these pages. Inevitably, the interpretation is a personal statement. Yet it is one arising out of a shared situation, so that I hope that I succeed in providing scope even for the reader who differs most widely from me to sharpen the focus of his own point of view. Now, as never before, no man is an island, and as we all share in common the problems of living in the modern world, it should be possible to arrive at a common understanding about the nature of these problems and the solutions to them. I hope, therefore, that this book will prove helpful both to those who ask: 'What is the use of studying history?' and, more generally, to those citizens of contemporary world society who seriously ask the question: 'Where are we going?'

The book has taken a long time to arrive at its present form, and I am deeply conscious of many debts incurred in the process of its gestation. I have tried to acknowledge my obligations to personal friends and acquaintances in the dedicatory list. Sadly, too many of those named are no longer able to receive my thanks. Others may wonder at – or be indignant at – their inclusion, and if so I can only say that I am aware of having benefited from my contact with them, although I would not care to particularise the nature of this benefit in all cases. Still, to all these I am grateful, as I am also to Mrs Judith Burchell and Miss Joanna Valentine for their help in preparing the typescript. And finally, my thanks to my wife, for her inspiration, support, and constructive criticism over the last thirty years.

University of Bath   R. A. BUCHANAN
29 September 1978

1. Introduction

The Nature of History

Man is irrepressibly inquisitive, and about nothing is he more inquisitive than his own past. For millennia, his ability to probe the past in order to discover his own origins was restricted by lack· of information. Apart from the physical evidence of earthworks and masonry which survived from earlier generations, he had to rely on the oral traditions passed on in his own kinship group, or upon the traditions of other groups with which he came in contact. Such traditions could be reliable guides to events within the previous two or three lifetimes, but beyond this time-barrier they merged into the legends of great heroes and the myths which poets and prophets had devised in an attempt to explain the mysteries of the past and of the natural world. In such folklore, the past was invariably fore-shortened, the primeval act of creation itself being envisaged as within a short time-scale of human generations, and the great events of the past – and, in some cases, its heroes – were considered to be still active agents in present and future events. Even the physical evidence which was easily available was interpreted as proof of the existence of gods or Cyclopean beings whose magical powers exceeded those of contemporary human beings.

The early civilisations of the second and third millennia BC did not easily escape the spell bound by their own legendary and mythological interpretations of the past. The priestly cults of Sumeria and Egypt accepted these 'stories' without reservation and reinforced them by the catalogues of conquests and other victories which, using the new skills of literacy, they began to record. The growth of these written records added steadily to the amount of information which was available about the past, but the way in which it was compiled did little to help towards a sound interpretation of past events. In this, as in so many other respects, the Greeks made the first significant contribution. They possessed their own powerful mythology of the past, with the gods on Mount Olympus ever ready to intervene in mortal events, and the legends of Homer's warriors inspiring successive generations of Greek children in the martial arts. But they also possessed the human quality of inquisitiveness to an exceptionally high degree, and in pursuing their enquiries into every branch of human knowledge they turned their attention to the problems of historical experience.

The first of the Greek historians was Herodotus. Writing in the fifth century BC he set out to assemble, as methodically as he could, the 'stories' of the various cultures around the eastern Mediterranean. He travelled extensively around the Aegean and Black Seas, and to Egypt and Persia, collecting information about life and customs, about past events and contemporary aspirations. On this basis he constructed his own appraisal of how the civilisation which he knew had developed, and gave a perceptive account of the background to the wars between Greece and Persia. This systematic reconstruction of what had actually happened in recent history was a drastic departure from earlier folklore and chronology, although Herodotus used both folklore and chronologies in compiling his history. His successors tended to react strongly to his methods: to some he became the 'Father of History', but others dismissed him as an inveterate liar. What was distinctive about the method of Herodotus was his determination to weigh the evidence he assimilated, checking it against other evidence, checking it for internal consistency, and checking it against standards of common-sense rationality. He still managed to make mistakes, as when he dismissed the evidence of navigators who claimed to have sailed round Africa because their report that the sun was on their right as they sailed from east to west seemed to him to be an unreasonable flight of fancy, and thus undermined the authenticity of their evidence. He also showed that, in matters of deference to oracles and other popular superstitions, he did not completely manage to shake off the mental blinkers of his own civilisation.

Despite all his weaknesses, the achievement of Herodotus was remarkable. He deserves the credit for inventing a technique whereby it has become possible to reconstruct a reasonably accurate interpretation of past events. Of course, the events with which Herodotus dealt were those of a comparatively recent past.

Depending, as he was obliged to do, on a large amount of hearsay evidence reported to him at first or second hand, he recognised the limitations of such evidence and made no attempt to extend his historical reconstructions into the more remote past except in the few cases such as his access to Egyptian priestly records which provided him with fairly reliable documentary evidence. In his willingness to combine evidence of physical, oral, and documentary nature, and to submit it all to the rigorous scrutiny of a critical mind, Herodotus demonstrated for the first time the true power of history to recover information about the past which would otherwise be lost beyond hope of recovery.

It would be reasonable to assume that, once discovered, the value of the historical method would not have been forgotten. But as well as displeasing many of his contemporaries, Herodotus has not been well received until quite modern times, with occasional exceptions such as Cicero, who was one of his Roman admirers. The preferred type of history amongst the Greeks and Romans was a catalogue of great events rather than a comprehensive reinterpretation of the past as attempted by Herodotus. Thus Thucydides, for all his narrative skill in reconstructing the events of the Peloponnesian War between Athens and Sparta, adopted a much more limited objective than Herodotus, although he also had perforce to rely largely on oral evidence and was prepared to resort to the imaginative embellishment of his leading characters when direct evidence failed him. The later Roman historians such as Livy kept even closer to the method of the chronological narrative, sticking together fragments of received evidence in what has been styled the 'scissors and paste' type of history. Occasionally, there were forays into a wider sphere of historical interpretation, as when Tacitus ventured on a general survey of the history and customs of the Germanic tribes. These, however, were the exceptions, and the rule remained a rather stylised and uncritical review of the political and military events of Roman history.

With this firmly established Classical precedent in historical studies passed on to Western Civilisation and adjusted to take account of the rise of Christianity, there was little incentive to adopt a more critical view of the available evidence. Although the volume of documentary evidence increased steadily throughout the Middle Ages, most of it enjoyed the prestige of ecclesiastical authority or the equally sacrosanct authority of the Classical masters, so that the task of the historian remained essentially that of piecing together the available fragments. The Venerable Bede managed to effect an excellent salvage job of this kind for the history of the church in England between the collapse of the Roman Empire and the seventh century AD in which he was writing. His general attitude, however, is heavily but understandably restricted by the authoritarian assumptions of his time, and by the current preoccupation with religious conversion, superstition, and the importance of making a good death as the necessary precondition for life hereafter. Such assumptions remained strong for another thousand years, and were prejudicial to the emergence of an objective science of history.

To speak of an objective science of history may appear to beg several questions. The consensus of modern historiography – the study of the study of history – is that complete objectivity in history is unattainable. Objectivity, indeed, has come to apear in the twentieth century as a god-like perspective which is unattainable by mere mortals. In this century of relativity, we have to choose between different degrees of relativism, but once this is recognised it is possible to approximate to what may be called relative objectivity in our study of history. This has become true, of course, for all disciplines, and not only history. Even the physical sciences have conceded the lack of complete objectivity and the principle of uncertainty in some form or other. This makes it all the easier to judge history by the same criteria as any other 'science': it is a pursuit of knowledge, conducted on the frontiers of our ignorance, proceeding by the systematic application of rigorous methods in the assessment of evidence and the construction of interpretations. Thus, even though historians have by and large abandoned the hope entertained by many nineteenth-century scholars of arriving at a final version of the past as it actually happened, they have still as much justification as any other discipline in considering themselves a branch of science.

While recognising the scientific basis of the study of history, it is hardly necessary to add that history differs significantly from other sciences, both 'natural' and 'social'. Unlike physics and other natural sciences, it is not open to verification by experiment: an historical event can not be replicated in a laboratory, under controlled conditions. Similarly, history is not concerned with the formulation of general laws (although there are some exceptions, as we will see) like the natural sciences or even some of the social sciences, such as sociology. Being concerned with human beings in their social relationships, history has much in common with the social sciences, and as all the basic information about society used in these sciences (sociology, economics, politics, psychology, anthropology, etc.) is historical in the sense that it is recorded information about past events, it is not being too extravagant to say that history is essential to the social sciences. Yet it differs from the social sciences, because.its primary concern is with unique, unrepeatable events, and not with the formulation of general rules which may or may not arise out of such events.

The boundaries between the sciences are thus not clearly drawn, and the study of history deserves a position among them. Not only is it a rigorous discipline, seeking truth according to a systematic method, but it also feeds necessary information to other sciences. Even some of the natural sciences have a substantial historical content, and it may be argued that the assimilation of this historical element was responsible for the tremendous scientific revolution of the nineteenth century when first geology and then the life sciences accepted the implications of evolution, of change over time. Admittedly, the new time-scale required to make sense of geological, botanical, and biological evidence, was so vast that it also involved the transformation of historical perspectives, because historians, like everybody else, had hitherto accepted the traditional view that the age of the universe could be measured in a few thousand years. Yet the discovery of the time dimension in the study of the natural sciences owes much to the growing historical perception of change taking place over a long time period. And in an even more fundamental sense, geology is an historical science because much of its evidence resembles that of historical documents: fossils have to be 'read' and interpreted as evidence of stratigraphy, and enable the reconstruction of past events in ways which are not capable of laboratory experiment any more than the unique events with which the historian is concerned. Perhaps mathematics and theoretical physics, the least historical of the natural sciences, need to discover such a time-dimension also. Certainly the confusion and intellectual absurdities which clutter the field of modern cosmology could be improved by a more careful application of historical principles to the evaluation of hypotheses.

However important it is to see history in relation to the other sciences, it is necessary also to retain a clear understanding of its links with other studies, and particularly with the humane studies of literature and philosophy. Historians have always valued good writing. Although they have not always managed to achieve this ideal, they have understood the need to communicate their historical reconstructions to their fellow human-beings, and thus to express themselves without resort to a specialist language and in a style that is lucid and readable. The best history has frequently been great literature, a point exemplified in British historiography by names such as Gibbon, Macaulay, Carlyle, Trevelyan, and a host of others. History is for people, and historians who forget this by writing for specialists or computers are quickly dismissed as poor historians. The converse, of course, is not necessarily true: the well turned phrase and purple passage may make good literature, but it is not history unless it incorporates disciplined research, selecting and assessing historical evidence.

History has another link with literature, because it is through the written word that the historian achieves an act of the creative imagination, converting a mass of undigested information into a carefully articulated and meaningful selection that impresses the reader by its inner cohesion and elegance. The nineteenth-century positivist historians hankered after an historical account which would achieve a complete recall of events for posterity. Thus Lord Acton advised his contributors to the first edition of the *Cambridge Modern History* that footnotes would not be necessary as each chapter would be as complete a summation as possible of all the available evidence. Historians now take the more relativistic view that complete recall, like complete objectivity, is not possible. Instead every historian is faced with the task of making the best interpretation of his chosen events, in the knowledge that he has to select from a vast mass of available information. The way in which he makes this selection will be determined partly by the sheer hard work of assimilating all the information which is likely to prove useful, and partly by the creative intuition which he brings to bear on this material. In this sense the historian is a creative artist, making the past live again in his imagination, and then conveying his insights to his readers.

The old argument about whether history is a science or an art is thus resolved: it is both. It is also a form of philosophy, in so far as it is concerned with a general interpretation of life in the past, and therefore, by implication even if not explicitly, of life in the present. Modern philosophy, it is true, has tended to play down these broader aspects of its role and to concentrate on very narrow questions of the meanings and use of words. These, also, are important for history, so that it is possible to interpret the philosophy of history at both micro- and macro- levels. The micro-philosophy of history is concerned with the verification of historical truth, the nature of historical causation, and related problems. The result of such investigations in the twentieth century has been to confirm the relativistic and subjective qualities of the study of history which we have already noted. But it has also established that the process of historical research, by the examination of 'documents' (Collingwood extended this term to include oral and physical evidence, although this needs converting into 'documentary' form before the historian can use it), and by the sifting of these in the historian's mind so that the pieces of information come to compose a coherent and internally self-consistent account, is a valid method of investigation, comparable with the experimental method of the natural sciences.

The macro-philosophy of history is concerned with the attempt by historians to make sense, not just of isolated events, but of the whole history of man. This raises some large and complex issues with which it is difficult to deal briefly, but as they are issues which are very relevant to the exercise undertaken in this book, they must at least be confronted. In the first place, it must be acknowledged that most professional historians are uneasy about any speculations which have the flavour of such a macro-philosophy of history. It seems to them that, in order to make such general speculations about the purpose of history, the historian needs to adopt a god-like perspective and that to do so is a pretension which modesty forbids them to adopt. Moreover, historians are very aware of the fact that, of those of their number who have dared to make Olympian speculations of this type, many have abused the opportunity to promote subjective opinions about race, climate, nationalism, and a wide variety of other hobby-horses. They have thus tended to become, at best, prophets with some new illumination about human destiny, or, at worst, salesmen pedalling a particular idea. In either case they cease to be historians. The caution of professional historians about being caught up in such philosophical speculation, is thus both understandable and justified.

Secondly, however, it should be realised that no matter how reserved the historian may be about such general philosophical speculation on the processes of history, he will himself possess such a philosophy. If it is implicit and unstated, it is likely to reflect the conventional wisdom and assumptions of his times. Nineteenth-century British assumptions about liberalism and constitutional government, for example, were taken for granted by most British historians of the century. These assumptions conditioned historians to choose particular subjects for examination, directed the way in which they selected significant evidence, and prejudiced their assessment of historical events. While such conditioning can be clearly discerned for periods other than one's own, it is difficult to isolate the features of the conventional wisdom under which one operates and to make appropriate allowance for it. But the difficulty of doing so is no excuse for not recognising the fact that we do operate within a network of assumptions, axioms, and beliefs, and that these amount to a tacit philosophy of history.

If we can, as historians, acknowledge that we are children of our own time, we should be able to take a further step and admit that some important questions such as 'Where is our civilisation going?' do admit of a sober historical treatment, without incurring the abuses of speculative philosophy of history which have already been mentioned. The question, indeed, is not itself an historical one, as it asks for a comprehension of the present and an understanding of the prospects awaiting our civilisation in the future. But it implies a series of vital ancillary questions, such as 'What are the origins of our civilisation?' and 'What is civilisation?' which may, more properly, be regarded as historical questions, and it is certain that we will not be able to determine where our civilisation is going without establishing adequate answers to these supplementary questions. The macro-philosophy of history with which we will be concerned, therefore, is an attempt to understand the dynamics of our civilisation, by taking a long view of history. Some historians have claimed to discern patterns and general laws in history, such as Oswald Spengler's vision of the decline of Western Civilisation, and Arnold Toynbee's mechanism of 'challenge and response'. We will be concerned less with such explanatory concepts than with an attempt to determine what actually happened in history to make our civilisation what it is. In so doing, we will inevitably have to rely heavily on the work of other historians, because the range of the operation precludes the possibility of any one person doing original work on all parts of it. The end of the exercise will be to achieve a sound historical foundation upon which it is possible to make projections about the likely, or at least the possible, course of future developments. But before embarking on this task of macro-philosophy of history, it is necessary to consider in more detail some of the problems of conducting such an historical enquiry, and to state as clearly as possible the objectives and assumptions of the enquiry.

The Future of the Past

History is, on any reckoning, a vast subject covering the whole record of mankind, and for our purposes it will be necessary to go back to the beginning of this story in order to trace significant patterns of historical development. To this extent we will be adopting the dangerous but unavoidable techniques of the macro-historians: dangerous, because it is impossible to avoid prejudice in world-embracing generalisations; but unavoidable because it is necessary to make general judgements, however tentative, in order to arrive at understanding, and it is understanding of the human situation which is the overriding purpose of this exercise. On the other hand, such understanding also requires the more discriminating judgement of the micro-historian, working on a minute segment of past ex-perience, and we will have occasion to call on this when detailed evidence is relevant. Even though there will never be a completely satisfactory and final interpretation of the human situation, because absolute objectivity and ultimate truth can never be attained in an historical reconstruction, the approximation of the historian to these ideals provides an indispensable foundation for our comprehension and thus for our understanding of present and future policy. This sense of 'applied history', of history being of practical use, is the best justification for taking the subject seriously as a guide to the prospects of our civilisation.

Not all historians would accept this argument of the utility of history as a reason for its study. There is a strong tradition of historical scholarship which has regarded the research exercise virtually as an end in itself, and which has expressed strong antipathy to any attempt to use the past as a means of providing the keys with which to unlock the mysteries of the present and the future. While I do not accept this view, I recognise that there are certain abuses of history into which it is easy to fall as soon as one begins to arrange discreet pieces of historical reconstruction into a pattern. It is necessary to be alert to these abuses, which may be considered under three headings.

The first is the abuse of chronological causation, according to which an event coming after another event is deemed to have been caused by the latter. Historical causation raises questions of philosophical complexity which do not concern us immediately: what is important to realise, however, is the far from simple relationship which exists between historical events in time. History is, in one sense, the study of human relationships in the time dimension, and the temptation to arrange a narrative in a sequence which is both temporal and causal is a strong one. Chronology – a sense of time – is an important part of the historian's equipment, but it should not be allowed to dictate links of cause and effect. Such links may exist, but if so they must be established by a close examination of the events. Except in the most general sense that every event has an influence on what comes after it, precise causal links in history can only be established with difficulty, and then only in a fragmentary manner.

The second historical abuse is whiggery. Sir Herbert Butterfield applied the term 'The Whig Interpretation of History' to a tradition of historical scholarship which he considered to be still fashionable when he wrote the tract of this title in 1931.[1] The Whig historians, on this view, had been guilty of ransacking the past in order to produce justifications for their contemporary moral and political judgements: it was a way of reading history backwards, with the preoccupations of the present uppermost in the mind of the historian. Butterfield called this the 'Whig Interpretation' because he illustrated it most forcibly from those historians of the British Whig-liberal tradition who interpreted history as the progress in inevitable sequence towards representative government and liberal democracy.

But the abuse has a more general relevance, as it can be practised by nationalists, or Marxists, or Fascists, or whatever ideological interpreters happen to be seeking historical justification. Whiggery, in fact, is any sort of partisan history. History is a big book, and can supply evidence for any imaginable point of view, provided only that the required 'facts' are selected sufficiently ruthlessly. Every party and interest group tends to do just this, making its own 'Whig interpretation' in order to bolster up its case. It is hard to see how it can be otherwise. The alternative to whiggery is not a 'Tory Interpretation', as that is only another partisan selection of the available evidence, but an interpretation which emphasises the irrational, contingent, purposeless, elements in history, and such a view is as much an abuse of the evidence as the most partisan whiggery. Nevertheless, the critique of whiggery has been helpful in warning professional historians of the dangers of indulging their own prejudices. That such prejudices exist should be recognised, but they should not be allowed to distort the historian's interpretation.

The third abuse is historicism. This is a difficult term, partly because it is used in a variety of different ways. Most historians prefer to avoid it completely. Others interpret it, like Professor Marwick, to mean 'historical geneticism' or a concept of history as 'a unified interconnected process'. Or others again, like Professor Plumb, take it to mean a sort of historical relativism. But the use which has to be taken most seriously is that adopted by Professor Karl Popper, who in a widely discussed essay, *The Poverty of Historicism*, defined historicism as 'an approach to the social sciences which assumes that *historical prediction* is their principal aim'.[2] Popper advanced trenchant philosophical arguments for rejecting such an approach, and it would be rash for an historian to challenge them. The historian may fairly observe, however, that the gravamen of Popper's critique is directed at those social sciences, especially sociology, which are anxious to acquire data for predictive purposes, and that historians rarely if ever venture into the prediction business.

Nevertheless, in the sort of interdisciplinary exercise on which we are here engaged, there is a temptation to demonstrate the 'use' of history as a means of forecasting the probable course of future events, and it is as well to be on guard against such forms of historicism. The history with which we will be concerned is an attempt to explain and understand the main lines of development of our own civilisation. In so far as it will provide us with some guidelines for making possible projections of future developments, we will be using it in a non-historical way, but the process of drawing out such projections is an important aspect of any responsible policy-making activity and is not to be confused with making predictions. A prediction is a precise statement of how things will happen, usually based upon the application of a general law. It is implicitly if not explicitly deterministic: we are told what is to be and there is no room for manoeuvre. A projection, on the other hand, is an open-ended possibility derived from a careful assessment of previous (historical) experience. It is likely to be fulfilled if conditions similar to those in which it previously occurred are repeated. But the historian knows that any sort of conditions will never be precisely repeated and that there is always a margin for human choice and idiosyncrasy, and that there are always alternative possibilities to whatever projections he ventures to make. Provided that these qualifications are kept firmly in mind, it should be possible to avoid the abuse of historicism.

The case I am arguing in the following pages is that at this time of phenomenal change in terrestrial societies, some of the best clues we can obtain about the future lie in the past, and can be made available by the study of history. History is a tremendous repository of human experience, and even though no two experiences are exactly alike, and the experiences of the twentieth century have in many respects no close precedents, it is only from this repository that we can hope to acquire the insights which we need to guide us in the present and the future. Professor Harold Perkin has argued that social history is a 'vertebrate discipline' in the sense that other studies need to be related to it like subsidiary bones to the backbone, and the claim can be generalised for history as a whole.[3] History can certainly supply such a disciplinary backbone to the social sciences, establishing their interrelationships and showing their relevance. Although, as we have seen, history cannot be categorised simply as a social science, it is none the less an essential prerequisite to the social sciences if they are to present any sort of cohesive interpretation of human experience for future use. From its unique 'data bank' the students of society, of politics, and of economics, can draw a wealth of precedents, parallels, and other clues to illuminate their interpretations. While the social scientist is concerned with understanding human nature and explaining the intricate structure of social problems, he cannot afford to neglect this fund of available evidence, and should he do so his studies will lack depth and interpretative significance. They will be as unrelated and irrelevant to each other and to reality as the bones of a skeleton without the backbone.

Objectives and Assumptions

This book, then, is an exercise in applied history. It springs from a belief that history has a practical use, in that a careful study of the past is essential to an understanding of the contemporary world and its likely development in the future. To many professional historians this conception of applied history is unacceptable, and nothing that I can say is likely to change their convictions. But it has long seemed to me that historians have a responsibility to apply such wisdom as they acquire in the pursuit of their vocation to the tasks of the citizen in the modern world, with all its perplexing problems. Surrounded by so much that is novel and unfamiliar, it is necessary to consult the tried and tested experience of the past in order to see the events of the present in a perspective which makes them intelligible. In the following pages I try to discharge this responsibility of the historian to make some sense of the confusion of his own time.

The recognition of contemporary confusion about the purpose and aims of our civilisation is the first step towards enlightenment. Modern Industrial Civilisation is the product of many centuries of growth. Now, in the second half of the twentieth century, it is confronted with a crisis, a crisis of a magnitude which is without parallel in human history. It has created the power to destroy itself, and possibly the entire human species, without having prepared a social and political structure which can guarantee its survival for even a single generation. We have been aware of this critical situation for three decades, and to restate it baldly thus is only to say again what has become a cliché of modern thought by virtue of frequent repetition. To restate the problem, moreover, is not to offer a solution to it, and it is a solution we need. If, indeed, a solution can be found – and it can by no means be taken for granted that this is possible – it can surely only be by making a careful analysis of the dynamic forces which have made our civilisation what it is, and by considering the objectives, both explicit and implicit, towards which these forces are driving. In the light of such an examination it should be possible at least to arrive at a clear understanding of the nature of our society, both past and present, and, more speculatively, to attempt some projections of the direction in which it is likely to move in the future. Such is the nature of the exercise presented in this book.

As the issues at stake concern the very survival of civilised life on the Earth, it is hardly necessary to justify this exercise. The remarkable fact is that *so little* attention has been given to the problem of survival in the years since the first atomic bomb explosion in 1945, in either academic or popular literature. Many studies have been made of particular aspects of the problem – international tension, political instability, social strife, ecological imbalance, and so on – but very few efforts have been made to relate these various aspects in a single survey of the forces which are moulding contemporary civilisation. Perhaps the multi-disciplinary breadth of the task has inhibited scholars and commentators from making this sort of survey. The modern tendency is towards increasing specialisation in all fields of study, so that it is now widely believed that only research on some hitherto unobserved or unexplored minutiae can have any validity. In the physical and life sciences it may be granted that most advances come from research of this nature, although even here it would be a serious error to ignore the significance of the comprehensive systems by which the greatest scientists have reinterpreted a mass of such detailed research by a new understanding or 'paradigm' of the nature and objectives of their study. In the case of the humane studies (those dealing with human beings in their creative and socio-political activities), however, the situation is rather different, due partly to the greater imprecision of human nature in comparison with physical forces and chemical substances, but mainly because of the lack of a universally accepted set of general propositions about their subject matters.

In the so-called 'social sciences' in particular there seems in recent years to have been an agreement to attend only to the trees and to leave the wood to look after itself. The result has been a proliferation of intensive detailed studies and a corresponding disregard for the overriding perspectives of human society. These studies doubtless have a certain validity within the narrow limits which they set themselves, although even this value is lost to some extent by the introduction of a highly technical vocabulary. This is not to imply that a technical vocabulary is always unnecessary: the microbiologist investigating the process of photosynthesis or the engineer seeking to improve the efficiency of the internal combustion engine both need a technical jargon. It is not so certain that jargon can perform a useful service in the social sciences, where the objective should be to explain society to itself, and to do so in a language which will be generally intelligible.

The purpose of these observations is not to denigrate the social sciences, which are frequently able to illuminate particular aspects of social behaviour or social policy, but to support the contention that these disciplines have failed conspicuously in recent years to make any contribution to the overriding problems of our civilisation. More positively, they are made in order to emphasise a different approach, which will be developed in the following pages, aimed at presenting an argument which is both multi-disciplinary and couched in the language of everyday communication. The multi-disciplinary nature of the argument is required by the wide scope of the subject matter, for it is necessary to consider the problem of survival from several points of view, although in all of them primary importance is attached to an historical perspective. As for the language of everyday communication, this is required in order to perform the exercise in terms which will be intelligible to anybody able to read English. Even the microbiologist and the engineer mentioned previously should be able to explain what they are doing in terms which the proverbial man-in-the-street can understand, although he cannot expect to grasp how they are doing it. In the case of the social sciences it should not be necessary to confront the intelligent layman with such a language-barrier, and he is probably right in suspecting that the use of technical jargon in these circumstances is an elaborate confidence trick, of which the first victims are the authors themselves. A primary aim of this essay is thus the presentation of a complex problem in common-sense terms, in the belief that the first prerequisite for a solution to the problem is that it should be understood.

This conviction that the central problem of our age can be stated in common-sense terms, without a cloud of jargon to make it unintelligible to all except a small group of readers, is the first of several assumptions which are made in the following pages. As it has already been argued that the selection of significant evidence and the quality of the judgement of every historian is inevitably influenced by his individual assumptions, beliefs, and prejudices, it is most desirable that the reader should be aware of them in the present exercise so that he can make whatever allowances he feels necessary. Most of them are assumptions which I share with my generation, but it is as well to realise that they are assumptions none the less. Perhaps my belief that complicated issues are capable of being expressed meaningfully in common-sense terms is not one which would be generally shared in the academic world, and represents one of my more optimistic aspirations. I hope, all the same, to be able to demonstrate it in the course of this essay.

My second assumption is that we are involved in a process of development: that the complex society to which we belong is evolving, that it has been evolving for the past thousand years, and that we can confidently expect a continuation of this evolutionary process in the future if only man can be prevented from destroying himself. The fact that this assumption is widely shared in the twentieth century does not detract from its importance as an intellectual presupposition. Until a hundred years ago, only a small minority of the population was accustomed to thinking in such terms so that the habit of evolutionary thinking has been recently acquired and it has therefore become a distinguishing characteristic of modern man.

I assume, thirdly, that the process of evolution is subject, in large measure, to human control. We are developing as we are because particular people have taken decisions and performed actions in the past which have produced results in the present, just as our decisions and actions will produce their consequences in the future. In other words, I reject fatalistic and determinist theories of social evolution, even though I recognise that there are many factors beyond direct human control, and that human actions do not always bring the consequences they intend. It has become fashionable in some literary and historical circles to bewail the subservience of modern man to technology, and to express the belief that the machine has now become the master over man. I do not accept this pessimistic view. In my judgement, even the most sophisticated machines are still the creation of men, and the uses to which they are put are still determined by men. It is a poor craftsman who blames his technology when things go wrong. I am an optimist about human capabilities, if not about human motives.

My next range of assumptions concerns the objectives of social evolution. I believe that certain social and political forms are more desirable than others, and that we should endeavour to achieve those which are desirable while avoiding those which are, in my view, less desirable or positively harmful. To be more specific, I believe that a structure of world government is an urgent necessity for the survival of our civilisation, that a democratic form of government is preferable to all others; that a 'good' society should aim at a high degree of social equality and social welfare; and that a 'healthy' society requires a sense of collective purpose and community. I attempt to justify these and other beliefs in the course of this book, but I begin with the admission that they *are* beliefs rather than scientifically demonstrable propositions. So anybody who approaches my argument with assumptions of, say, ardent nationalism or a deep conviction in the benefits of autocratic government, will not find them congenial reading. I hope, nevertheless, that he will still consider the arguments, and be converted.

In using words like 'good' and 'healthy' in connection with social structures and human performances, I am making value judgements implying another set of assumptions which I should declare. My views on moral-ethical priorities are broadly those of the mainstream of Judaic-Christian-Humanist values which have figured prominently in the aspirations of Western Civilisation, even if not always in practice. I accept, that is, the high valuation of human personality which derives from this mainstream tradition, with its corollary, the belief in the brotherhood of mankind, according to which individuals of every race, colour, and creed are entitled to liberty and the exercise of responsibility. I accept, moreover, the insights associated with this tradition regarding the frailty of human resolutions, the mixture of human motives, and the instinctive animal impulses of human nature which are never far beneath the sophisticated skin of civilisation.

While admitting that I start with certain assumptions, and that I am trying to work out their implications in this book, I am not attempting to put the assumptions beyond the pale of discussion. Even the most firmly-held assumptions are subject to the erosion of argument, the discovery of new information, and the maturing effect of long familiarity, so that I would be claiming to be more than human if I considered my assumptions, however basic, to be immutable. If I were to write this book in 1988 instead of 1978 I might have modified some or all of my presuppositions. But this is my standpoint in 1978, and certain consequences stem from it. We are, after all, dealing with a set of intensely real situations and problems, and unless we – we, that is, as the human species – find some solutions to these there may be no 1988 for anybody to write a book from any standpoint. I am writing now because I am convinced that there could be a long and creative future for our species – provided that we take certain steps in the near future to control our own destiny.

The concept of destiny is unfashionable today, perhaps because it has been frequently used in the past to justify wars of conquest and other barbaric activities. I suggest, however, that it is a useful idea, because it indicates a mutual interaction between the forces which have moulded our civilisation and the decisions of the living representatives of that civilisation. Destiny, as I understand it, is not a fatalistic concept, but involves a large element of human choice. It is choice, however, operating within limitations: it is made on the basis of a given situation and comes into conjunction with other forces and human choices, many of which are unpredictable. But human choice is a vital factor in forming the future, and even if people contract out of the responsibility towards the future, this itself is a choice, and they have only themselves to blame when the 'natural' forces, which is to say those resulting from 'normal' or 'predictable' human choices, take place. Our destiny is thus the interaction between the past and the present – the given situation and the act of choice – which moulds our self-determined future. Our destiny, in short, is not to be read in our stars but in our own resources of vitality.

2. Society and Civilisation

One of the great difficulties about teaching history to children is that most of them have little sense of time. For them events are immediate and memories are short: the happenings of the previous year are already remote, the childhood of their own parents seems incredible, and the existence of a more distant past is almost inconceivable. People in simple societies perpetuate these attitudes into adult life, but because human curiosity is infinite even though information is non-existent, the past beyond a few known and remembered generations is populated by legendary heroes or by myths of creation and renewal. Such societies have no sense of history, but in its place they have folklore, myth, ritual and magic. History only began, as we have already observed, with the systematic attempts by Herodotus and other Greek scholars to recover evidence of the past. This attempt required both rigorous standards in discriminating between good evidence and bad, and an imagination capable of grasping the significance of change over time. Only a well-informed and inspired imagination can make sense of the past, in the literal meaning of arranging it in a pattern that is sensible or meaningful.

It is worth reminding ourselves of the imaginative component in history because it is an intellectual faculty which is too easily taken for granted or – much worse – forgotten. Without it, the teaching of history is barren, losing its sense of movement in time and becoming a purposeless narrative of facts, sometimes reduced to the ultimate absurdity of a list of dates of reigns and battles divorced from any attempt at meaningful interpretation in a context of chronological development. The genuine historian, in contrast with this sterile approach to the past, is in a real sense a 'time traveller', capable of thinking easily in the dimension of time because he possesses the imaginative qualities which enable him to recognise relationships and to interpret information about past events. The scope for such historical reconstruction has gradually increased as the information available to the historian has grown, but until quite recently there was no reason to think that this body of knowledge could be substantially enlarged beyond the earliest documentary evidence dating back no further than two or three thousand years BC. Beyond that, after all, it was universally held that the Creation occurred by divine fiat around 4000 BC, so that there was effectively only a little gap between the periods of recorded history and the beginning of time – a belief which illustrates neatly the typical foreshortening imposed by ignorance.

Ignorance only began to be dispelled in the nineteenth century, when the intellectually explosive qualities of discoveries in geology and the life sciences wrought havoc with the previously unquestioned time-scales of world history, and when archaeological evidence began to accumulate of human developments stretching back over much greater periods of time than any previously considered or even conceived. The intellectual revolution which followed has been aptly described as 'the discovery of time', and has added tremendously to the scope of human history. In some academic circles the notion survives that the only genuine history is that of recorded events, but ever since Professor Gordon Childe set out forcefully a generation ago to tell us *What Happened in History* by calling on archaeological and anthropological evidence to review the whole development of the human species, this traditional view has declined in favour.[1] We have no difficulty now in recognising that history is as old as mankind, although it is realised that for most of the time-span of the species the only available evidence is of a physical quality and that fully-fledged documentary history is a luxury of the comparatively recent past. With this new vantage-point we are able to see the rise of our own civilisation against a backcloth of long-term human development.

The Beginnings of Civilisation

Man-like species, culminating in our own *homo sapiens*, have almost certainly existed on this planet for two or three million years, and the recent research of archaeologists in central Africa seems to be steadily pushing back in time the origin of such species. But however much it is extended, this period will remain only a minute fraction of the vast eons of geological time which preceded it, from the formation of the earth about 4,500,000,000 years ago. These astronomical calculations are obviously somewhat arbitrary, but the latest work of cosmologists on the evolution of the universe and of our own star, the sun, and its family of planets, suggests an order of this magnitude. The universe is, indeed, very old and very large, in ways which we are still not able to comprehend, and its ultimate mysteries of time and creation are as yet almost completely obscure to us. Yet man has shown remarkable capacities for extending his mental horizons, and it is not too much to hope that, given time, he may one day be able to plumb the depths of even these mysteries.

Meanwhile, our concern here is primarily with the last few thousand millennia during which man has existed on the earth, and particularly with the last few hundred years of his spectacular evolution. Our knowledge of our remote ancestors during most of this period is necessarily fragmentary in the extreme, but enough has been reconstructed by the patient skill of the archaeologists for us to make some tentative generalisations.

It is reasonably certain, for example, that man was a rare species for most of this period, consisting of a very few small groups inhabiting tropical and sub-tropical lands where food could most easily be collected and where warmth-giving clothing was unnecessary. It is equally certain that his life was extremely precarious, consisting of a perpetual struggle for existence in the search for food, and with man being a constant prey to animals stronger than himself. The fact that man survived at all was due to his adaptability, his ingenuity, and his assiduity. He was better able to adjust to changes of climate and habitat than any other animal, so that in time he settled all over the terrestrial land masses and applied himself to a wide range of occupations. His ingenuity showed itself in the tools, the weapons, and the techniques which he developed. The primitive technology of the Old Stone Age ('Palaeolithic') included the control of fire, the manufacture of stone implements, and the invention of the bow and arrow. These gave him increasing prowess as a hunter and thus contributed substantially to his mastery over other species. Man's assiduous application to the business of survival, involving forethought, planning, and patience, marked his superior intelligence over other animals and was, perhaps, his greatest asset.

Even in this protracted period of barely perceptible development, man created distinctive social and cultural organisations. It is reasonably assumed that the basis of these organisations was the family, and that there was a rudimentary distinction of function between the men, who were usually the hunter-warriors of the community, and the women, who were normally the home-makers and child-rearers. A degree of specialisation certainly existed in the communities whose cave paintings have survived, and it is likely that the artists of these often skilfully executed drawings were fulfilling ritual functions. Evidence from the burial mounds which occur so widely over the British countryside also demonstrates that, by the end of the Old Stone Age at least, human beings had begun to wrestle with the problem of death by making ritual provision for the departed members of the tribe.

Mention of the tribe emphasises an assumption which should, perhaps, be made more explicit. Man is a gregarious animal for the simple reason that he depends on his fellow-men for his survival. The human child requires at least ten years of nurturing before he or she is able to begin taking an adult role as a member of the group, whether this be the simplest form of two-parent family with one child or a much more complex social organisation. In either case, the child is an involuntary member of society, and although in certain 'Robinson Crusoe' circumstances an adult individual can survive alone, such societal dependence remains a characteristic of human life. *Society* is thus the primary concept of human organisation. A society is a group of human beings who are doing something together. The common object in which they are united may be something fundamental like survival or bringing up a family, or it may be some more contingent goal such as a ritual activity or an exploratory expedition, but in any event the society depends for its continued existence upon the desire or the need for human beings to join together for some specific purpose. Despite the ability of men and women to form widely variegated, overlapping, societies in order to fulfil their physiological and psychological requirements, however, all societies are to some extent artificial. Even the most hallowed societies such as the family, the state, and the church, were at some time the creation of one or a series of bargains, conquests, or promulgations. The capacity for modifying his social organisation has, in fact, been one of man's most productive inventions. The simple tribe, being an extension of the family unit, served the needs of man throughout the Old Stone Age, but the transition to a more sophisticated régime required a concomitant development in the social organisation. The tribe thus became larger and more complex, with specialised functions more clearly defined.

With the ending of the last Ice Age in the Northern Hemisphere there appears to have been a growth in the human population, and as climatic conditions became increasingly favourable in the river-valleys of sub-tropical latitudes, so the larger population devised new techniques for achieving subsistence. Some ten thousand years ago, communites in these regions began a slow but definite transmutation to a new way of life, which was to be so decisive for the future of the species that it has been called 'The Neolithic Revolution'. Throughout the preceding period of the Old Stone Age, man had gathered or hunted his food. Now, in the New Stone Age, he began to learn how to cultivate his own food and to domesticate animals as livestock. With this transition to an agricultural or pastoral way of life, human communities became more settled and increased in numbers. New skills were acquired and, because communications between groups had improved, were passed on and embellished. The processes of pottery-making and fermentation were developed, and clothing was made from various natural fibres which had been spun into yarn. With the growth of these skills specialisation increased, although it seems likely that most of the new skills were practised by women while men remained primarily warriors.

These important innovations of the New Stone Age took place in the warm, forest-free, fertile river deltas of the Middle East and India, where conditions were most favourable for the regular cultivation of crops and grazing of animals. They gradually spread up the river valleys as the techniques of irrigation were acquired. It seems probable that these developments occurred spontaneously once the basic skills of food-growing and animal husbandry had been grasped, as we know that similar processes took place in China and, somewhat later but even more isolated, in America. By the end of the New Stone Age, around 4000 BC, the concentration of population in these favoured areas was beginning to assume something of an urban character, and the transition from settled agricultural society to civilisation could begin.

Civilisation began with the conjunction of several important factors. The natural increase of population in the fertile river valleys of the Nile, the Tigris – Euphrates, the Indus, and the Yellow River, together with the production of a food surplus through the techniques of systematic agriculture, stimulated the concentration of population in towns, where the surplus could be exchanged for the products of specialist craftsmen. A particularly important development was the discovery of the first metallurgical techniques for working copper and bronze, and the impetus which these gave to the growth of highly skilled crafts, and to the trade necessary to obtain the raw materials for them. These skills associated with metal working became specialised activities of men rather than women in most of the societies which acquired them. The need for accurate calendars and methods of measurement in order to predict the seasons and to control trade led to the first systematic use of numbers and encouraged the development of another male-dominated specialisation – the priest-clerk, using his skill in numbers and literacy to read omens, to predict eclipses, and to fulfil various ritualistic functions. The invention of the wheel and the plough, the increasing use of the horse, and improvements in ship construction, all contributed to increasing productivity and trade. By the beginning of the third millenium BC such factors had combined to transform the Neolithic agricultural communities of the Middle Eastern river valleys into genuine civilisations.

Here we must pause to decide what we mean by a 'civilisation', as this concept is second in importance only to that of 'society' in understanding the nature of human history. A civilisation is a large and complex social organisation: one which is effective over an extensive territory and over a period of time measured in centuries rather than decades. It is distinguished from primitive societies by the sophistication of its institutions, involving a high degree of functional specialisation amongst its members; by social stratification; and by the mastery of literacy and numeracy. Civilisation is self-conscious and articulate: it records its achievements in words as well as in physical remains. The historical records of many civilisations are known to us, showing great divergences in the details of their organisations and objectives, but all of them have shared certain basic features, without which civilised life could not long be maintained.

The first general characteristic of all civilisations is a highly developed system of wealth creation. The production of a surplus above that necessary for life-support is essential to the existence of civilised life, and represents the fundamental difference from the subsistence economy of a primitive society, in which all the resources of the society are committed to a perennial struggle for survival. A civilisation must be able to produce an excess of material wealth, particularly food, over its immediate requirements, so that at least a minority of the population are freed from the total involvement in survival. The process of wealth creation thus becomes organised (agriculture, industry, trade, etc.) and gives a powerful dynamic quality to civilisation because it is never complete: the arrival at one stage of productive efficiency is only the prelude to a further expansion. If the process slows down or stops, it is likely that the civilisation is collapsing. A civilisation is always threatened with the prospect that it will revert to more primitive conditions, and it is a matter of historical fact that many highly developed societies have collapsed in this way. When the Roman Empire disintegrated, for example, the whole of Western Europe relapsed into the conditions of a comparitively primitive economy for six centuries. Imaginative writers have had no difficulty in depicting a similar return to such an existence in the event of an atomic war in our own time – assuming, of course, that the species survives such an ordeal.

The second general characteristic of a civilisation is some sort of political or cultural cohesion which unites its members against all outsiders. This quality is sometimes elusive. Not all civilisations possess political homogeneity such as that dictated by the Egyptian pharoahs or Byzantine emperors, where the rule of one man was unquestioned over the whole territorial limits of the civilisation. The more normal political pattern has been one of heterogeneity, such as that of Ancient Greece with its multitude of city-states, and that of the diversity of nation-states in Europe since the fifteenth century. In these cases, however, the monolithic quality of single-state civilis- ations is replaced by racial, linguistic, or cultural bonds which exercise a similar cohesive influence. The Ancient Greeks were thus united by the possession of a common language, in contrast with which the non-Greek speaking 'barbarians' deserved their name because they sounded as unintelligible as sheep. There has been no comparable linguistic unity in Western Europe, where half a dozen major languages have developed and maintained their identity, but there have been more subtle springs of cultural cohesion in common religious traditions and in similar expansive aspirations, even when these have been accompanied by bitter inter-state rivalries. As over against the encroachments of Slav, Mongol, Turk, and Moor, the citizens of Western Civilisation have mustered sufficient cultural identity to put up a united, even if sporadic, resistance, and on occasion there have even been attempts to give some form of political reality to this sense of oneness. But that is to anticipate our account, and here it is only necessary to make the point that even a civilisation so diverse and apparently divisive as that of modern Europe has in fact possessed strong bonds of cultural affinity.

Provided that the formula for successful wealth creation has been discovered and a sense of cultural identity acquired, civilisations develop other common characteristics. Perhaps the most obvious visual feature of a flourishing civilisation is the proliferation of town life. For a variety of reasons, the process of wealth creation encourages a concentration of population. Increase in food supplies stimulates a rise in the population, and the requirements of security and convenience in marketing are attractive advantages of towns. Then as towns grow and the processes of production become more complex, the growth of crafts and manufacturing industries further increase pressure towards urbanisation. Thus the walled market town near a strategic fortification grows into a large city and, in more recent times, cities merge into vast conurbations.

It has been persuasively argued by Jane Jacobs recently that the city is so vital a factor in the growth of civilisation that it precedes development in the surrounding countryside, the latter only being stimulated into activity by the presence of the city and its demands for food, raw materials, and a market.[2] It certainly seems to be a general pattern of urban development that whenever a town acquires facilities for commerce and production, it can no longer be regarded as an agrarian village in which the population is predominantly engaged in the fields, but becomes a centre for specialised urban activities and as such a focus of civilised life. It has long been a truism of economic and social existence that the more the processes of wealth creation can be broken down into their simplest parts, with each part allotted to a particular group or individual, the more efficient the processes will be. In a static, rural, society, the amount of specialisation is minimal. Every family attends to the production of its own food and clothing, tools, weapons, and essential buildings, and in an emergency every able-bodied person will be called out to the defence of the community. To some extent the local ruler or tribal leader, the village priest, the blacksmith, and the miller, will have specialist functions to perform, but within the self-contained community this will not have much effect on productive capacity. In a civilised society, however, specialisation in production is essential to continuous wealth creation, and is systematically organised. It is frequently represented by an intricate caste and craft social structure, which defines the functions of all members of the society in relation to their particular specialisations.

Specialisation goes hand-in-hand with trade, because the various specialists need to exchange their commodities, and thus a flourishing commercial activity with an elaborate monetary system of exchange is another general characteristic of civilisation. Trade is also necessary in order to acquire raw materials and commodities not available near at hand, and is an important feature in the expansion of civilisation. A good example of this process was the enterprise of Bronze Age merchants in seeking out and exploiting sources of tin in the first two millennia BC. Tin was needed for the copper-tin alloy called bronze which was in great demand for weapons, tools, and ornaments amongst the wealthy citizens of the eastern Mediterranean civilisations. Being a much rarer metal than copper, tin was highly prized by the bronzesmiths and elaborate trading relationships developed to meet their needs, which included the creation of trading settlements in the western Mediterranean and voyages out beyond the Pillars of Hercules. The development of trade routes frequently resulted in improvements in roads, ships, and other forms of transport, and these derivative benefits frequently had important military and expansive consequences. Trade, in short, acts as a powerful dynamic agent for change and growth both within a civilisation and in its relations with its neighbours.

A final general characteristic of civilisation is the nexus of 'civilised' qualities implied by literacy, numeracy, advanced artistic creativity, sophisticated religious ritual, and systematic attempts to observe and explain the natural environment. All these may be conveniently comprehended in the word 'clericalism', because they are all associated with the work of a privileged, leisured, class of literate people, whether these are priest-clerks, as in many early civilisations and medieval Europe, or lay academics, as in Classical Greece and modern Europe. These are the people who, usually only a small minority of the population, sustained in comparative leisure by the surplus production of the majority, have articulated and recorded the aspirations of their societies throughout the centuries of civilised life. Even more than the merchants, the clerics have been responsible for the transmission of civilised culture and ideas, and hence for the expansion of civilisation itself. Clericalism in all its forms has been the most distinctive and potent aspect of civilisation, as it is by its achievements in art, literature, architecture, sculpture, religion, and science, that the finer nuances of civilised life are judged.

The Dynamics of Civilisation

The presence or absence of these features – wealth creation, cultural cohesion, urbanisation, specialisation, trade, and clericalism – enable us to define the existence of civilisation and to distinguish some sort of sequence of civilisations in the historical record. The dynamics of this progression of civilisations are exceedingly complicated, and in any case we lack the factual information necessary to reconstruct a completely accurate account of the process. In very general terms, however, it is clear that there are two aspects to consider: the internal 'life-cycle' of a civilisation, and the external relations between civilisations. The life-cycle of a civilisation seems to begin with the discovery of a successful formula for wealth creation, leading to the achievement of an appreciable surplus of food production over immediate needs. This stimulates an increase in population, the development of town life, and the beginning of a truly industrial specialisation. The need for raw materials to supply the craftsmen and for luxuries to delight the ruling classes encourages trade. Knowledge of other territories gained through trade, a consciousness of cultural superiority over neighbouring people, and the pressure of population at home, combine to promote expansion through colonisation and conquest. The period of expansion is generally accompanied by a phase of comparative prosperity at home, and by vigorous cultural and intellectual activity. When the economic and technological limits of expansion have been reached, the prosperity is maintained for a time by the tribute of subject people and by the use of slaves taken in conquest for all heavy duty and menial tasks. The use of slaves, however, leads to the hardening of class distinctions in a way which concentrates wealth more and more in the hands of a small ruling group, and to the neglect of the agricultural and industrial techniques on which the wealth of the civilisation was originally based. Cultural activity, also, becomes less popular and more restricted in this phase. High taxation persuades craftsmen and merchants to take their skills elsewhere. Neighbouring groups are strengthened by the arrival of such immigrants, and their envy of the civilisation increases just at the time that the latter becomes more vulnerable to attack, with the result that the civilisation is either rejuvenated by the imposition of a new dynasty from outside, or is completely overthrown by a qualitatively different civilisation.

It is not suggested that every civilisation follows this pattern of evolution in detail. The process has varied greatly in different cases according to the problems and opportunities of the natural circumstances encountered by each civilisation, the direction of its expansion and conquests, and the qualities of its leading personalities. Nevertheless, every civilisation previous to our own has passed through these phases of consolidation, expansion, ossification, and collapse, so that it is not irrelevant to look in the records of these civilisations for precedents even if we consider that our own case is in some respects unprecedented, as it undoubtedly is. It may be possible to control the internal dynamics of civilisation, but only if they are properly understood, and it is here that historical analysis is potentially valuable.

There is a similar justification for studying the external aspects of the relations of one civilisation with another. The dynamics of these relationships are many times more complicated than those of the internal life of a civilisation, but again, as with the life-cycle of a single civilisation, there is a basic pattern to be discerned. The earliest civilisations emerged from primitive societies in the third millennium BC, in Egypt, Mesopotamia, India, and China. Archaeological investigation has done much to elucidate the nature of this transition, even though documentary evidence is non-existent. These early civilisations, except for that of the Indus valley which expired without direct successors, were extremely stable by more modern standards, undergoing occasional rejuvenation rather than complete destruction. This was probably due to the compactness of their fertile lands and the regularity of their seasonal changes. The later civilisations of the eastern Mediterranean – Phoenician, Minoan, Carthaginian – relying for their prosperity as they did on a thriving commercial activity rather than any domestic fertility, were much less resilient, and the same was true of classical Greek civilisation.

These were all second-generation civilisations, in the sense that they all derived from the primary civilisations rather than directly from primitive societies, and from the second millennium BC they were expanding westwards around the Mediterranean. In the third

century BC, Alexander demonstrated that military skill could establish a large empire out of disparate pieces of primary and secondary
civilisations, and the Romans exploited this technique further to
unify the whole of Mediterranean civilisation in one political unit for
several centuries. But eventually the internal processes of ossification
and collapse reasserted themselves within the Roman Empire. The
fall of Rome to Alaric's Goths in AD 410 became the symbolic event
marking the disintegration of the Western Empire and the reversion
of the Roman provinces to a more primitive condition of society. The
way was thus open for the emergence of third-generation civilisations
in Western Europe, and also in the eastern Mediterranean where
Byzantium, the 'Second Rome' based on Constantinople, gradually
lost ground before the onslaught of the new Islamic civilisation.

Meanwhile, in China, a series of gigantic displacements took place
over many centuries as one dynasty replaced another in virtual
isolation from western influence until the nineteenth century. These
dynastic changes corresponded to changes in civilisation, masked to
a large extent by the continuity of Chinese languages and of the
Mandarin clericalism which emphasised the uniformity rather than
the diversity of successive epochs of Chinese history. But the basic
internal pattern of the life-cycle of civilisations can still be recognised
underneath this apparent uniformity, as it can in the nineteenth-
century collapse of China when confronted at last by Western culture,
and in its subsequent rejuvenation in the present century. The other
significant non-Mediterranean civilisations were those of America.
These appear to have developed spontaneously in the first millennium of the Christian era, although ingenious attempts have been
made to demonstrate the feasibility of contacts with Old World
civilisations. The civilisations of the Aztecs and Incas were probably
already past their peak when they were destroyed by the Western
invaders in the sixteenth century, but the evidence suggests that the
American civilisations had previously followed the same sort of
evolution as those in other parts of the world.

Various attempts have been made to explain both the internal and
the external dynamics of civilisations. Amongst the latest and the
best known is the monumental work of Arnold Toynbee in *A Study
of History*.[3] Toynbee distinguishes a total of some twenty-eight
civilisations, which he divides into the categories of primary,
secondary, and tertiary, which we have already adopted, and which
involve in his analysis definite developments by transmission and

refinement between one level and the next. The element of human choice is preserved in Toynbee's system by the mechanism of 'challenge and response', according to which every civilisation meets a continuous series of challenges, caused either by external factors (invasion or environmental changes), or by internal tensions (oppression and class conflict), and the quality of its response will depend upon human action or inaction which will determine the subsequent stage in the development of that particular civilisation. Toynbee has supported his thesis by a mass of detailed evidence drawn from a remarkable range of sources, but as traditional historians, who have no taste for such macro-historical studies, have been ready to point out, the trouble with this sort of argument is that there can never be sufficient evidence to justify the sweeping generalisations encompassing the whole of human experience to which it leads. It is always possible to find exceptions to any generalisation of these dimensions, and historians have applied themselves with enthusiasm to criticising the minutiae of Toynbee's thesis. But the central principles of the thesis are well sustained, and I accept them in this essay. They establish that there is a development of civilisations, produced by the transmission of ideas and institutions from one to another, and that the element of human choice is important in determining this development. The outstanding characteristic of this position is that it is not deterministic. It resists the temptation to draw the conclusion from the study of past civilisations that they go through an inevitable cycle, and that on this model our own civilisation is at present moving into the phases of ossification and imminent collapse. Some commentators have placed great emphasis on this 'Decline of the West', and it is impossible to say that they are completely wrong. But the Toynbee thesis provides grounds for hope, in that it allows scope for a creative response to the challenges which face our civilisation. This civilisation has already developed in ways which are qualitatively different from those which preceded it. It has become the first fully industrialised civilisation, exercising world ascendancy and possessing unique powers of destruction. Whatever the future may hold for our civilisation, therefore, it is sure to be extraordinary in the sense that it will bear little resemblance to anything that has happened before.

In discussing the dynamics of civilisation we have been using concepts like 'evolution', 'development', and 'progress'. We should be clear what value we give to these terms. They are being used in what is primarily an organic sense of change from a comparatively simple form to one which is more sophisticated. In this sense, an oak tree 'develops' from an acorn, and a mammal 'evolves' from invertebrate creatures. 'Progress' is a more problematic idea because it is frequently used with a sense of moral approval. There can be no doubt that in terms of material achievement there has been measurable progress over recent years: people travel further and faster, communication has become instantaneous: more wealth is produced than ever before. But the moral aspects of such progress are less measurable: it is by no means clear that it is good to be able to travel faster, and there is no certainty that the greater wealth available is any better distributed than it was previously. Nevertheless, it must be recognised that there has been great hope attached to the idea of progress, so that the idea is something which has to be reckoned with in any understanding of the contemporary world. What is important is not whether or not material progress has been achieved (which it has), or moral progress cannot be discerned (which is questionable), but whether or not men believe in progress. And here it must be said that, for better or for worse, progress has become a universal aspiration of twentieth-century man. The citizen of an advanced European society does not mean the same thing by progress as a peasant in a developing country, but they are united in the belief that it is a good thing, and that it must be sought after. Belief in progress, indeed, has become a substitute religion for man, and is not to be lightly dismissed. So even though we can study the 'progression' of civilisations in the sense of acquiring greater organisational complexity and wealth-creating capacity, it is necessary to reserve some use of the word progress to denote one of the great formative ideas of our civilisation, and one which has contributed in no small measure to the dynamic quality of our own society.

3. The City and the Individual

The primary civilisations of Egypt and Mesopotamia grew slowly and in virtual isolation from each other or any outside influence until the second millennium BC. Then internal developments and continued expansion brought them into contact along the 'Fertile Crescent' from the Tigris–Euphrates through Palestine to the Nile, and from contact stemmed trade, rivalry, and conflict. The second millennium BC was thus a time of increasing activity between the major civilisations and of subsidary groupings which eventually emerged as distinct secondary civilisations. In Persia to the east, Anatolia (Asia Minor) to the north, and along the coasts and islands of the Mediterranean to the west, vigorous new societies arose with strong roots in the-primary civilisations but with a will for independence which helped them to develop their own cultural identity and so to emerge as secondary civilisations. The eastern Mediterranean had considerable advantages for this sort of development. The sea provided both a challenge to enterprising merchants who knew that there were rich mercantile prizes awaiting those who could master it, and a barrier against too much oversight from the parent civilisations, amongst which sea-faring did not figure as an outstanding accomplishment. So the new civilisations, thriving on the basis of rich trading relationships, were left to fend for themselves, which some of them did with great success. Around the coast and on the islands of the Aegean Sea, in particular, new cultural patterns were established towards the end of the millennium, with the Minoan culture of Crete and the Mycenean culture of mainland Greece and Homeric legend prominent amongst them.

These cultural stirrings of the second millennium BC were largely the product of the trade encouraged by a Bronze Age society, and bronze was the outstanding metal of all the civilisations of this period. But early in the following millennium, techniques of working iron began to spread from the Middle East and these initiated a series of significant changes in Bronze Age cultures. For one thing, warriors armed with iron weapons were better equipped than those with the comparatively soft metal bronze, so that the Iron Age tribesmen who moved southwards into the Greek mainland were able to invade and settle successfully and to lay the basis of Classical Greek civilisation which came to fruition in the sixth century BC. Being an abundant metal compared with the non-ferrous ingredients of bronze, iron was, also available for a wide range of uses, although weaponry for long remained its major application. But it became possible to equip whole armies with iron swords, daggers, and so on, instead of only the leading warriors. Even so, there was as yet no large-scale production of iron, as every piece of wrought iron had to be made by a laborious process of heating the ore in a small furnace, normally using foot-powered bellows to create an adequate draught, and then hammering the red-hot 'bloom' of spongy iron taken from the furnace in order to consolidate it into workable iron. Only very gradually did the secret of giving this iron the right carbon content to make high quality steel emerge, so that the best swords made with this metal assumed a legendary character, like the 'Excalibur' of Arthurian legend. Nevertheless, the fact that iron at least was widely available meant that every man in Roman legions could be armed with an iron weapon and partially protected by iron armour.

The first great civilisation of the Iron Age was that of Classical Greece. Acquiring distinct cultural identity in the sixth century BC, this flourished for some three centuries, after which it passed through conquests and expansion into the orbit of Roman power, but the influence of Greece remained so strong that it is reasonable to include the period of Roman supremacy with that of Classical Greece as 'Hellenic Civilisation'. This survived effectively until the fourth century AD, so that it can be said to have endured for a millennium, although in a transmuted form it continued for another thousand years in the Eastern Roman Empire of Byzantium. This combination of Classical Greek and Imperial Roman in Hellenic Civilisation was a typical secondary civilisation. It derived directly from the primary civilisations of Egypt and Mesopotamia, and eventually incorpo-rated them. But it also possessed qualities of profound originality which, in a different topographical and racial context from those of the primary civilisations, served to give it very different cultural characteristics. As many of these characteristics were eventually passed on to those tertiary civilisations which followed, including our own, it is well worth examining the Hellenic heritage for clues towards an understanding of our own civilisation.

The Greek City-state

The salient physical fact of Classical Greece was its diverse and fragmentary character. Scattered over the hundreds of Aegean islands and the adjacent coastlines of Asia Minor and mainland Greece, there could be little unified administration or political control. Blessed with a comfortable climate, the Greeks were never the less neither able to rely on the fertility of regularly enriched river valleys to support them with the necessities of life, nor were they well endowed with natural resources which could be exchanged for these commodities. Instead, they had to depend on their own wits and skills, producing pottery and other manufactured goods to supplement the olives and silver which they were able to exploit, through an elaborate trading system. The miracle of Classical Greece is that it survived at all in these precarious conditions, and lived out one of the most exalted and profound experiences of mankind. The political organisation which enabled them to do this was the *polis* – the city-state. There is no precise English equivalent for the Greek '$\pi o \lambda$ is', but 'city-state' is the closest approximation. The *polis* was certainly more than the city, although the walled city with its central defensive bastion or acropolis was essential to its existence. But every city administered a hinterland of territory or islands, possibly including other towns, and in some cases these dependencies became veritable colonies or part of an empire. The *polis* was thus a state as well as a city, and it was to the Greeks the only form of state fitting for a free man. Barbarians or members of other cultures like the monolithic Persian empire, which was for long their nearest neighbour and rival in the east, may be better off in other sorts of state, but for the Greek only the *polis* was an appropriate form of life.

The state is such a crucial concept of political discussion that we should be sure that we know what we mean by it. The state is a particular sort of society, and as in any other society, the members come together for a specific purpose. In the case of the state, the common purpose is defence. Defence is two-sided. Internally, it consists of the maintenance of social cohesion, of establishing a regulated order of life in which the members of the community can go about their business, protected from molestation by the sanctions of rules backed up by an efficient police force. Externally, the defensive function of the state consists of its resistance to attack from outside, which makes necessary some provision of armed forces and sometimes involves a readiness to attack neighbouring states in defence of interests, real or assumed, of the state. These two functions remain the same however much the state may alter in size or shape, from the nomadic tribe to the city-state or the nation-state. They are the essential functions of sovereignty – of the supreme political powers of self-regulation and self-defence in default of which the state society will forfeit its cohesion and integrity.

From this analysis it will be clear that the state is not necessarily a territorial institution, occupying a given plot of ground. In effect, however, the establishment of settled communities led to states defining their territorial frontiers in relation to their neighbours. Like nature, states abhor a vacuum, and the existence of a no-man's-land in its vicinity has always been regarded by a state as a weakness or as a justification for expansion. In either case, the available empty spaces have all been occupied, so that the states of the world have assumed a strongly territorial character and become identified with local cultural, ethnic, and linguistic traditions. This process had only just begun amongst the city-states of Classical Greece, so that the sense of linguistic and cultural unity was still stronger than the divisive forces, despite the intense rivalries that developed between them. In our sense of the term, however, the Greek city-states were fully states, being completely responsible for their own internal cohesion as law-abiding communities, and for their own defence against any external attack.

Perhaps it was because of the diversity of political experience between the variety of Greek city-states that the thinkers of Classical Greece produced the first sytematic studies of political organisation. Other people have, however, experienced similar diversity without bringing to bear on it the brilliance and perception which were such distinguished qualities of the leading Greek minds. It is not merely that, in the popular adage, the Greeks 'had a word for it', although the devastating truth of this can be quickly seen by examining the origin of our key political and social terms. Something even more important is involved. It is not exaggerating to claim that the Greeks invented conceptual thought. Other men had thought long and hard in earlier civilisation to produce intricate irrigation systems, magnificent buildings, observations of the heavenly bodies, and other significant achievements. But most of this work had been of a particular, down-to-earth, quality, being concerned with the individual 'trees' of this or that project and rarely if ever with the conceptual 'wood' which related them to a common framework of ideas. The Greeks distinguished the wood from the trees for the first time, and they did so with such extraordinary clarity that in many respects there is little improvement to be made on their perceptions. Their analysis of political forms illustrates this splendidly. They recognised that the pattern of political organisation covers a spectrum between rule by one person (monarchy) through rule by a few and, it is to be hoped, the best (aristocracy), to rule by all the people (democracy). Tyranny represents a corrupt form of monarchy, and oligarchy a degenerate form of aristocracy, while anarchy, the condition of no-rule, represents a breakdown of democracy.

Having established these basic political concepts, the Classical Greeks were able to relate all their multifarious experience of political systems to them and to argue endlessly about the rival merits of different forms of government. It may appear that all this discussion did them no good, and that while the philosophers engaged in conceptual speculation the individual city-states of Classical Greece either destroyed each other or were conquered, first by Alexander and then by the Romans. But the language of all subsequent political discourse has been enriched by these Greek concepts, and that would have been a great achievement for any civilisation. With the Greeks, however, it is only part of a much wider achievement, for the conceptual facility which they applied to politics was applied also to the rest of society, to mathematics, to science, and to art. Philosophy begins with the Greeks, because they invented the habit of thinking about thought. Historical study begins with the Greeks, because they were the first people to ask systematic questions about past experience. All this, moreover, is without taking into account the aesthetic achievements of Classical Greece, in its buildings, sculpture, literature and art, which still bears favourable comparison with any other human civilisation.

We will have cause to return to several of these pioneering efforts of the Greeks in order to understand subsequent developments in our own civilisation, but in order to avoid considering the Greek achievements only at the level of generalisation it will be worth illustrating the account with one particular instance – that of Plato's *Republic*. This is the best known of the series of tracts which Plato wrote about the basic principles of social and political life. Like all of them, it is cast in the form of a dialogue, a discussion between Socrates, whom Plato remembered as his own master, and a group of his students. The argument is frequently lively and entertaining, even though punctuated by long monologues from the mouth of the master, and this gives the dialogues a dramatic quality which sustains their immediate interest. *The Republic* is the longest of Plato's dialogues, and is about many things. Explicitly, it is concerned with the definition of justice, Socrates eventually winning acceptance for the view, after he has demolished several notions submitted by his students, that justice is the right ordering of society in the sense that everybody performs the role for which he is best suited. By implication, however, it is also concerned with arguing that the best sort of government is that by a monarch who is a 'philosopher king', and with establishing the procedures whereby such a ruler is selected and trained, and by which the rest of the population are educated to perform their allotted roles. But overwhelmingly the dialogue is about the power of conceptual thought: the famous parable of the cave, in which Socrates describes the ineffable beauty experienced by the man who escapes from the mental gloom of dwelling amongst crudely perceived sense impressions and superstitions to see the full light of the midday sun, is best interpreted as a paean of praise for the intellect. The whole of Plato's work is inspired with enthusiasm for the ability to solve all problems by intellectual speculation, and the enthusiasm is infectious, so that a modern student coming fresh to *The Republic* can still enjoy the exultation of feeling that he is unlocking the mysteries of the universe by the power of thought alone.

Of course Plato was frequently wrong in his judgements. He often reached his conclusions on the basis of inadequate or faulty information, so that his arguments are open to detailed criticism. It says much for the strength of his arguments, however, that even in the twentieth century they are considered worthy of such detailed criticism by some of the most able philosophers of our day. Professor Popper, for instance, has traced aspects of modern dictatorship from faults in Plato's thesis in *The Republic*.[1] Yet even if there are senses in which this is true, Plato's elevation of the human intellect remains as telling in its force as when it was first uttered. This is one of the elements which are common to Classical Greece and the modern world, even though there are also cultural differences which should not be ignored either. The most striking of these differences is in relation to individual freedom. The Greeks had a powerful sense of the independence and freedom of their city-states, and as citizens of the *polis* the Greek individual could hope to participate in this freedom. But there remains a strong element of fatalism in Greek thought about the individual. The modern reader is perplexed by the authority which even so robust a Greek author as the historian Herodotus gives to the divinations of oracles, and even in the most sublime passages of Plato's intellectualism there is a readiness to subject the individual to the necessities of the rhythms and harmonies which constitute the ultimate Being of his universe. To the Greeks in general, the individual was in a real sense the plaything of the gods, at the mercy of fatalistic forces against which he might struggle heroically but to no avail. In a sense, too, the execution of Socrates by his fellow citizens of Athens was not because he persuaded the young to ask too many questions, but that he called in doubt the fatalistic beliefs which were part of the fabric of the Greek understanding of the universe, and in which the role of the individual could only be fulfilled through membership of the state. Even Plato, it may be argued, did not fully comprehend the implications of this offence.

The Rise of Rome

Socrates lived in the fifth century BC, the great age of Periclean Athens, and was executed in 399 BC. His pupil Plato was the teacher of Aristotle, who was in turn to become the private tutor of Alexander. When Alexander died in 323 BC, at the age of thirty-three, the great epoch of the Greek city-states was over. The most powerful of these states, Athens and Sparta, had already almost destroyed each other in the Peloponnesian War of the fifth century BC. This made the military progress of the Macedonian kingdom relatively easy on the Greek mainland, so that Alexander was able to use it as a base from which to conquer Asia Minor, Syria, Egypt, and Persia, unifying them for a short time into an empire which has inspired every suceeding would-be empire-builder. The first to copy the model were the Romans, who did so to enormous effect. Emerging as an important city-state in the fourth century BC, Rome achieved ascendancy in the western Mediterranean by her eventual victory over the Carthaginians in the Punic wars at the beginning of the second century BC. Thereafter Rome extended its territorial power by stages into the eastern Mediterranean, and completed the establishment of a worldwide empire by the time of the assassination of Julius Caesar in 44 BC. Up to this point Rome had maintained a republican form of government which permitted a remarkably high degree of participation by the Roman aristocracy and citizens, but the achievement of such a vast empire had created intolerable pressures within the republic so that it was replaced by an emperor ruling with absolute power, except in so far as it was necessary to preserve a power-base in the army. This form of government endured until the collapse of the Western Empire in AD 410, and even survived it to undergo several rebirths in name, if not in substance.

It is frequently contended that Rome added little to the cultural heritage of Hellenic Civilisation, as the great achievements had already been made by Classical Greece, and that Roman culture was imitative rather than creative. There are sound reasons for accepting this judgement, in so far as the Romans rarely if ever reached the level of conceptual sophistication which was characteristic of Greek thought at its best. But the comparison is really not a fair one. In the first place, Rome suffers by its proximity to Classical Greek culture in time, for as we have seen the Greek achievement was so remarkable that no other single culture can bear favourable comparison with it, and in taking their architectural and artistic models from the Greeks the Romans were only doing what many subsequent cultures have done. And secondly, it should be remembered that Rome created the political conditions for many of the achievements of later Hellenic Civilisation. Ptolemy and Galen, for example, two of the giants of ancient science, whose works were regarded as the repository of wisdom for over a millennium, both flourished in a society under Roman political domination. The Romans, indeed, deserve credit for an outstanding political achievement. They had a genius for government, and they created a system of administration backed by clear laws and an efficient army and supported by the necessary works of civil engineering such as roads, harbours, and aqueducts which brought peace and good government to the whole Mediterranean world for 500 years. While the Greeks had destroyed each other in internecine conflict, the Romans established peace and the conditions necessary for settled trading relationships, industry, and commerce. The *Pax Romana* must be numbered amongst the great achievements of civilised societies.

The wonder is, in retrospect, that so little of permanent value came out of this prolonged period of settled government. The administrative system became increasingly devoted to the business of raising revenue, most of which, in the form of taxes, found its way back to Rome, leaving the provinces comparatively impoverished. The support of a substantial leisured and consuming society in the capital city itself, added to the expense of maintaining the legions in a condition of military preparation, became an oppressive burden stifling the initiative which could, if directed into wealth-creating activities, have done much to alleviate the problem. Instead, however, trade languished in the later Roman Empire, while industry and technology made significantly little progress. Even the legal system, which can rightly be regarded as one of the great Roman gifts to mankind, was not universally effective during the period of the Empire. It was codified by Justinian in the sixth century AD, while the Western Empire was crumbling into dust, and Roman Law only became the widely acknowledged basis of European legal practice after the Empire itself had disappeared.

The collapse of the Roman Empire in the West has long presented historians with a conundrum, as there appears to be so little overt reason why such a powerful administrative-military system should go into liquidation. But the causes of this collapse can be identified, and although they might seem individually weak if the Empire had only to contend with them one at a time, they were cumulatively overwhelming. The increasing costs of the army, due in part to changes in organisation and recruitment, became a serious burden on provincial resources, but were justified by the continuing pressure on the long land-frontiers of the Empire which was not lessened by a policy of assimilating some of the encroaching barbarians and even using them as a source for military units. Meanwhile, the increasing demands of the central government in both Rome and Constantinople placed unrelenting pressure on the provincial administration, and the administration itself tended to become ever more bureaucratic and inefficient. In these circumstances the scope for trade and industry diminished, and, perhaps most serious of all for the stability of the Empire, resentment against government in general became widespread amongst the western provinces. In a sense, the

Empire collapsed because the great majority of its citizens had lost interest in keeping it intact. The reward for throwing off the burdens of Imperial administration and taxation was half a millennium of political chaos in which Western Europe forfeited such manner of civilised life as had been built up under the Roman Empire. But this consequence was not apparent to the citizens of the late Western Empire, who had lost their will to sustain the system. No political system, however monolithic and efficient, can long survive this sort of withdrawal of support by the people it purports to govern.[2]

The Roman Empire, it has been suggested, conquered the world three times: first with its legions, secondly with its law, and third with its church. Our account of the Roman achievement has been concerned so far with the military conquest and with the long period of political stability and good government which stemmed from it, but we have also indicated the influence which Roman law was to have on European legal systems. So far, however, we have said nothing about Roman religion in general or the influence on Roman culture of Christianity in particular. The culture of a society is its way of life: the things it does and the way it does them. This, at least, is the anthropological understanding of culture which is accepted for most purposes in this essay, although it must be admitted that it is easy to slip into the habit of using the word in a 'high culture' sense to denote the fine art, music, and aesthetic sensitivity of a society. On either interpretation, however, religion is a powerful factor, for it both influences the general way of life of a society and produces distinctive artistic forms which may make a significant contribution to the achievement of a society. Religion is about the aims of a society, about its goals, its eschatological concerns. Usually these concerns are expressed in terms of divine or supernatural guidance, but increasingly in modern societies they have taken strongly secular forms as in the case of materialist ideologies which determine precise secular goals for the aspirations of society. The Romans, like the Classical Greeks from whom they borrowed so much of their cultural equipment, had an ambivalent attitude to religion. On the one hand, their administrative and legal systems recognised a measure of human responsibility. But they rarely escaped from dependence upon an ancient and pertinacious belief in fate: in most important events of life, at least, the Romans believed that a man's lot was predetermined and that there was nothing he could do to avoid this fate. The ambivalence of classical thinking on this matter of individuality made it at first receptive to Christianity, because the new religion appeared to clarify some aspects of the problem. But the implications of Christianity for classical religion were shattering, and set the course of Western belief about God and man on radically different lines from those which had been previously followed. In so far as the Roman Empire adopted Christianity, and the Roman Church went on to represent the religion of Western Civilisation, there is some truth in the view that Rome conquered the world for a third time with her church. But it is also possible to interpret the same sequence of events as the conquest of the Roman Empire by a new religion, the implications of which helped to loosen the fabric of the Empire and to hasten its collapse.

The Responsible Individual

Out of the desert, a millennium before the birth of Christ, came a people with a new religious idea. In an epoch when gods still proliferated in every seasonal event and daily act, requiring constant propitiation and consultation, and having the fate of mortals completely in their charge, the people of Moses appeared from the wilderness of Sinai and, inspired by their vision of their God and confident in their choice by Him, they annexed a state for themselves in Palestine. Their God was not like other gods. In the first place, He was above all other gods: He alone was all-powerful and all-knowing: no graven image could represent Him because He was everywhere and at all time: above all, He was a Holy God, a mystery so overwhelming and sublime that mortal man could approach Him only in utter submission. Here, for the first time, the powerful religion of monotheism found full expression. But the God of Moses was not just an intellectual abstraction, a 'first principle' or a 'first cause'. He was Yahweh – a personal God, who had chosen His people, who had spoken to them and continued to speak to them, who was jealous for them and angered by their misdoings, but who was ready to be merciful and forgiving when they recognised their offences and repented. This conception of a personal God who loved His people but who exercised judgement over them and was prepared to chastise them, was as extraordinary as it was unique. No other society appears to have arrived unaided at such a profound and revolutionary concept. Under its influence, both the primitive propitiation rites of animism and the more sophisticated cynicism of fatalism were replaced by a dynamic religion which set goals for man's aspiration and achievement and which made him responsible to God for their fulfilment. If he failed to perform his personal task, the individual could no longer plead bad luck or fate: he could only confess his inadequacy and ask God, in His mercy, to let him try again. The individual, as a fully conscious and responsible entity, was the product of the Hebrew belief in God.

The religion based on the wilderness experience with Moses – and there can be no reasonable doubt that a historical person of genius lies behind the legendary accounts associated with this name[3] – has remained for 3000 years a potent force in world history. Judaism is the oldest of the 'higher religions', and several of the others derive from it. It remains a powerful and problematic political reality in the world today, having reoccupied the ancestral home in Palestine in the twentieth century. As the religion of the Hebrews, however, it has never been an evangelical religion seeking to win converts, and its conflict with Roman authority demonstrated its inability to influence the quality of Roman culture. Even though extrapolated onto a wider, cosmic scale by the prophets of the Exile around the fifth century BC, Judaism never managed to throw off the narrow tribal conception of the chosen people and to regard the divine choice as being extended to all races. This was the transmutation which was achieved by Christianity. Under the influence of Jesus and his followers, Hebraic monotheism and the conception of a merciful and loving God who expects men to behave responsibly and judges them accordingly, became available to everybody. Exclusiveness was replaced by inclusiveness, and the adherents of the new faith, coming from the prevalent Hellenic culture of fatalism and some forms of state-worship, found that they became free from the mental restraints of their time and felt themselves responsible individuals for the first time. The faith, indeed, could make men free.

Christianity, of course, did much more than this, and not all it did was potentially or actually as beneficial as this generalising of the Hebrew experience of individuality. In some respects, for instance, the intense Greek philosophising about the person of Christ and the nature of the Trinity obscured the simplicity of the Christian gospel and created a minefield of controversy which became deeply divisive as soon as the early Christian communities began to form permanent institutions. These institutions, in an attempt to maintain some particular terminological formulation of the faith, quickly became exclusive and militant towards the 'heretics' who disagreed with them, and the result has been centuries of destructive conflict about issues which could never have occurred to the mind of the founder. Institutional Christianity has been a disappointment in terms of the basic goals of Christian religion. But enough of these goals survived the rapid growth of Christian churches in the later Roman Empire, and even its adoption as the official state religion in the fourth century AD, to make it a significant political force in the critical centuries of Roman decline. Even though Christianity probably brought greater integrity to the administrative system at this time, it seems likely that the influence of the new Faith in weakening the family-state basis of Roman religion, and in turning the attention of its adherents away from secular concerns, made its contribution on balance one which hastened rather than retarded the collapse of the Empire. And when the collapse came, the church based in Rome with an organisation throughout the western provinces was the only institution to survive the débâcle, able to pass on traditions of Hellenic Civilisation to civilisations yet unborn.

The Hellenic heritage, then, was a rich and diverse mixture. A millennium of continuous civilised life had started with the most amazing explosion of intellectual activity which the world has ever witnessed, and which has left, besides its incomparable aesthetic legacy, a skill in conceptual thought to which every succeeding generation of Western man has referred for inspiration and guidance. This intellectual activity was generated within the political organis-ation of the city-state, an institution of which the Classical Greeks were inordinately proud even though their pride did not prevent them from coming near to destroying it. The Romans, a less imaginative but more practical people, assimilated the Greek experience of the city-state and generalised it into a system of imperial administration and law to govern the world-state which they constructed around the Mediterranean, achieving thereby a period of peace and stable government for five hundred years. In the long run, however, their imaginative inadequacy let them down, as they sacrificed the possible benefits of industrial and commercial expan-sion to the immediate tasks of bolstering up a military régime which the existing economy could not afford. The result was a collapse of civilised life, at least in the western provinces which were most vulnerable to barbarian attack. In this collapse, the widespread adoption of Christianity with its emphasis on individual responsibility played an important part, but also served to ensure that something survived the ensuing catastrophe. Greek ideas, Roman organisation, and Hebraic-Christian individualism were thus all available as models for the aspirations of later civilisations.

4. The Rise of Western Civilisation

The term 'Western Civilisation' is used in this book as a convenient label for the early stages of the civilisation to which we belong. The prefix 'Western' is not intended to be narrowly topographical or ideological, but refers to the Western European heartland, around the western Mediterranean and Atlantic seaboard, in which this civilisation arose. It also indicates a historical affinity with the territory of the Western Roman Empire, over against the more wealthy Eastern Empire centred upon Constantinople and the eastern Mediterranean. This Eastern Empire survived as 'Byzantium' until the fifteenth century, and when it collapsed there were other civilisations to the east which justified the continuance of the concept of a distinct 'western' civilisation. Only in the last two centuries, with the rapid industrialisation and world-ascendancy of our civilisation, has it become potentially ambiguous to describe it as 'western'. Modern China, Japan, and India, have all been profoundly influenced by Western Civilisation, and particularly by its techniques of industrialisation, so that the geographical antithesis between east and west has ceased to have any significance in this respect. So we switch to the usage 'Industrial Civilisation' to describe this most recent period, in order to suggest the greatly increased scope of our civilisation. But there is an essential continuity between the 'Western' and 'Industrial' phases of our civilisation, which will be apparent in this and the following chapters. Our civilisation has had about a thousand years of uninterrupted development, and in this chapter we will be concerned with the first half of this period, from about AD 1000 to 1500. During this period Western Civilisation acquired a self-conscious identity and evolved through a long process of more or less isolated growth. There were slight external influences, as we will see, but for the most part Western Civilisation was allowed to consolidate and become self-confident without major challenges from outside.

Our aim will be to isolate the main trends in this process of social evolution: to study, that is, the internal dynamics of our own civilisation in the early stages of its development.

The Origins

The roots of Western Civilisation must be sought in the so-called 'Dark Ages', when the western Roman Empire had crumbled away and been replaced by a comparatively primitive tribal system. This period of some six centuries was 'dark' in the sense that the lights of civilised life – urbanisation, specialisation, literacy, and so on – had been extinguished, and existence for most people had reverted to a struggle for subsistence. The period is also 'dark' in the sense that the paucity of written records makes our knowledge of it far less complete than that for the Roman Empire before it or for the new civilisation which followed it. Yet the period was not one entirely of loss. During these six centuries our civilisation established its distinctive racial and linguistic patterns, and there occurred that fusion between the tribal culture of the 'barbarians' and the traditions of the Christian Church and of Roman Law which has been of such great significance in the history of the world.

The economic and political organisation of Western Europe during this seminal period from the fall of Rome to Alaric in AD 410 to the last of the Viking incursions in the eleventh century can be summed up in the word 'feudalism'.[1] The term has been used in a number of different ways: to denote particular legal relationships and forms of land tenure, amongst other things. It is being used here in a general rather than a particular sense, to represent a self-sufficient, small-scale, agrarian society. Thus a feudal society is one which supports itself militarily and economically. It provides its own food by the cultivation of the land; it provides its own clothing, tools, and services; and it provides for its own defence. Each such society is in effect an independent feudal state, and Western Europe was splintered into a myriad states of this type by the barbarian invasions. Being self-supporting, each state carried on little trade with its neighbours. It had little need for money, as internal exchanges could be fairly easily conducted by barter. Towns were virtually eliminated, the only exceptions being military encampments at strategic points which occasionally, at convenient places, gave protection to a small local market or fair. Feudal society was a society in a defensive posture. Thrown back on its own resources, it had to protect itself against its rivals and the elements, or perish. It was almost completely preoccupied with the problem of survival.

For all this, the feudal states of the Dark Ages were not the same as the tribal communities which preceded the development of civilisations. The aura of Imperial grandeur survived the departure of the Roman legions, so that feudal societies retained a vestigial framework of Roman law and organisation. This was most evident in the network of personal relationships associated with possession of land and culminating in the person of one man who was responsible for leading a feudal state in battle and for maintaining law and order. Such feudal kings were more than tribal leaders: their authority was frequently buttressed by the religious sanctions of the Roman Church, which showed remarkable versatility in adjusting to the situation of feudal society and which, as the provider of a ready-made literate class and administrative systm, could endow rulers with a dignity greater than that which derived from their secular power. This distinctive feature of feudalism is outstandingly well illustrated by the establishment of the Carolingian Empire with the crowning of Charles the Great as Holy Roman Emperor by the Pope in Rome in the year 800. The 'Empire' of Charlemagne was in fact a motley conglomeration of feudal states held together by the personal allegiance of their rulers to himself, and despite the solemn ritual of consecration and coronation which revived the office of emperor it proved to be completely incapable of holding the Empire together after his death. Confronted by a further spate of invasions from the east, the Carolingian Empire dissolved again into its feudal components. But the Roman Church continued to spread the principles of good administration and to prepare the way for larger and more powerful groupings. And perhaps even more important, the ideal of imperial unity had been rekindled in Western Europe which, although transformed from the provinces of the western Roman Empire, was sufficiently receptive to the old traditions to seek to recreate old wine in the new bottles.

The Church was, almost unconsciously, performing another invaluable function. In describing the processes whereby the traditions of a secondary civilisation are passed on to a tertiary civilisation, Arnold Toynbee has emphasised the importance of the 'higher religions' in performing what he vividly expresses as the 'chrysalis' function. In the gestation of Western Civilisation, which fits neatly into Toynbee's category of being a tertiary civilisation, the Roman Church acted as the mediator of many of the institutions, ideas, and traditions of Hellenic Civilisation. It performed this function partly by incorporating some of these features into its own organisation and teaching, so that it was a working model of the old order. This was achieved both through the diocesan system which was in origin a survival of Roman provincial organisation, and through the rigorous order of the new monastic communities such as those established all over Western Europe on the Rules of St Benedict, with their Roman spirit of organisation and discipline. But even more significant was the role of the Church as the repository of books and other documents which would not otherwise have survived the collapse of civilised life. In episocopal and monastic libraries – if such a grand title can be used to describe what was often only a single box or chest – were preserved texts of the Greek and Latin masters which, although frequently fragmentary and bowdlerised, served to whet the intellectual appetite of the literate minority once the new civilisation began to look hopefully for the recovery of Hellenic culture.

By the end of the tenth century, Western Europe was passing from the predominantly defensive attitude of feudalism and beginning to form strong, expanding, communities. The latest barbarian attacks had been repulsed in Central Europe, and territory previously lost to the Slavs was being regained and colonised. In the north of Europe, the Vikings were at last being contained or assimilated. The nuclei of the future states of Western Europe were already in existence, although scarcely yet conscious of themselves as national units, and had established relatively peaceful and law-abiding conditions within their borders. European society stood poised on the brink of the expansive movement which has continued, with steadily increasing momentum, down to the present day.

Medieval Expansion

Social growth is a composite process, in which it is virtually impossible to isolate any one factor and to place it in a causal relationship to all the others. The development of Western Civilisation between AD 1000 and 1500 is a case in point. The cessation of the

Viking attacks with their successful establishment of settlements in the West, in Normandy, Sicily, and elsewhere, resulted in the spread of comparative peace and stability throughout the region. This made possible the development of trading relations, while improvements in agriculture associated with the three-field system on the manorial farms, new crops, and the harnessing of the horse, made a surplus of food available for exchange. Trade began hesitantly, and only gathered confidence as the internal security of Europe became assured. Then trade routes appeared, along the Rhine and the northern plain of Europe, and fairs were held at convenient places for the annual marketing of regional products.[2]

The growth in the volume of trade gave an incentive to the development of towns, which gradually superseded the fairs as centres of trade and encouraged the manufacturing crafts to take root within the security of their walls and municipal privileges. The increasing availability of manufactured goods – cloth, tools, ironwork, leatherwork, and so on – as well as raw materials such as wool gave a further stimulus to trade and increased the importance of the towns, which sought additional privileges for themselves through the acquisition of a charter from the local ruler, in return for the promise of loyalty and financial assistance. The rising number of financial transactions, meanwhile, had broken down the simple barter economy and created a need for reliable coinage. This need provided, in turn, an encouragement for stronger government, as only a well established government could mint and maintain a sound currency, and such a government could thus rely on the support of the vigorous groups with an interest in trade and industry. The appearance of such groups, coming between the aristocracy and the peasantry of feudal societies, marked the birth of the 'middle classes' even though the term was not coined until long afterwards. Thus strong states with relatively centralised systems of government were able to replace the local administrations and jurisdictions of feudal society, and to increase the area of peace and security within which the process of social growth could flourish. The process was both circular and cumulative: a step forward in any part of this complex set of interrelationships assisted the development of all the other parts.

Medieval Europe, then, whilst remaining predominantly rural, experienced the beginnings of urbanisation, specialisation, and the other characteristics of a civilised society. The towns which sprang up in this period were, to begin with, only large villages, and they functioned as extensions of a rural economy. But with their steady growth and acquisition of corporate status many of them achieved that independence of the immediately surrounding countryside which distinguishes a true town from a village. This transition was accelerated by the emergence of manufacturing industries in the towns, typically organised on the pattern of craft guilds. The guilds consisted of closely-knit fraternities of master craftsmen and journeymen (workmen employed by the masters) in one trade, together with the apprentices who were being initiated into the craft. They exercised a comprehensive control over the conditions of work, craftsmanship, and marketing in their trade, and they were also active in the social life of the towns, endowing churches and taking part in festivals. Such associations came into existence in all the new towns of Western Europe – in Northern Italy, the Rhineland, Flanders, and elsewhere – differing from place to place in accordance with local political and social conditions, but having the same basic features in common. They were the first stage in the development of modern industrial organisation, eminently suited to the conditions of a small-scale economy in a strongly ethical society.

The ethical consciousness of medieval society deserves special attention. It was the great achievement of the Christian Church in the Middle Ages, and the source of its enormous power, that it succeeded in impressing on the communities of Western Europe the importance of common ethical standards, and of its own authority to enforce these standards. The Church laid down rules of government, warfare, commerce, and industry, and maintained for several centuries the power to enforce them. The high standards of the craft guilds were one indication of this power. In many ways, the position of the Church in the Middle Ages was unique and anomalous. It claimed to represent a spiritual authority over and against secular authorities, and because of its virtual monopoly of literacy and learning, in addition to its sanctions of salvation and damnation, this claim was at first accepted without question. The Church was thus the great unifying force of medieval society, giving rise to the concept of 'Christendom', of a community possessing common beliefs, values, and objectives, which dominated medieval culture in all its aspects. Under the influence of the idea of Christendom, the role of separate sovereign states was muted, although not entirely absent, and Western Europe assumed the characteristics of a distinctive new civilisation.

The anomalous feature of medieval Christendom was that it failed to establish a political unity commensurate with this cultural unity. The major reason for this failure was the division of political authority caused by the claim of the Church to supremacy over all temporal powers. In the early stages of western political development this claim had been implicit rather than explicit, because of the mutual dependence of the Church and the incipient states on each other in an unstable environment, the Church needing the protection of law and order, and the new states needing the clerical skills of literacy and administrative competence which only the Church could provide. The Church had thus encouraged strong rulers like William I of England, and had helped them to increase the efficiency and centralisation of their governments, while itself benefiting from the alliance in wealth and increments to the prestige and authority of the papacy. However, in the more settled political conditions of the twelfth and thirteenth centuries, the Church attempted to transform its spiritual authority into an active form of temporal power, asserting ultimate political sovereignty over the new states. This claim created severe stresses within medieval society, and led to prolonged conflict between the Church and the new states, as represented partially in England by the struggle for power between Henry II and Thomas-à-Becket. The results of this struggle were significant, involving the drastic curtailment of the authority of the Church, the destruction of the unity of Christendom, and the splintering of political power in Western Civilisation which has been one of its most outstanding features ever since. Some commentators have discerned the genesis of European liberalism in the choice offered between the spiritual and temporal claims in this medieval conflict. But it seems more realistic to recognise in it the defeat of the first pan-European movement in Western Civilisation.

While the political authority of the Church was being challenged and curtailed by the states which it had helped to create, its moral authority was being undermined by the very process of medieval expansion which it had done so much to encourage by promoting stable and efficient administration. In the period of its greatest power, between the eleventh and thirteenth centuries, the Church took as its social ideal a pattern of life which was characteristic of the late stages of feudalism – a static, rural, society, in which everybody knew his position and contributed towards the common good. For this reason, Church leaders found many features of the changing society – the bustling towns, the growing social mobility, and the aggressive individualism of the merchants – unsettling and potentially dangerous. This attitude was reflected in canon law – the rules of practice laid down by the Church – and in particular in the condemnation of usury, or lending money at interest. In the eyes of the medieval Church, usury involved taking advantage of the misfortunes of one's fellow men, and was consistently condemned. No attempt was made to distinguish between the cruder forms of financial exploitation in what might be called the 'pawnbroker-poverty relationship', and the more sophisticated sort of transaction of the 'banker–client relationship' by which a well placed investment could bring profit to all the parties taking part in it. Official Church policy thus sought to frustrate any form of capitalist enterprise, and thereby incurred the opposition of powerful groups emerging in politics, trade and industry.

Capitalism is the process of accumulating surplus wealth and using it as an investment in commercial or industrial enterprises to produce more wealth. In the most general sense it is the key to the process of wealth creation which is amongst the prime instigators of development in a civilised society, although it may take a variety of different forms according to which social groups initiate it. In some civilisations it is the clerisy which controls the processes of wealth creation, but as this social order usually has a vested interest in the *status quo* it rarely applies itself with vigour to promoting these dynamic forces. More frequently, wealth creation is initiated by new social groups trying to establish a place for themselves in the social order, and so it was in medieval Europe. There was a widespread need for capital from the tenth century onwards, felt by merchants as their trading enterprises grew more ambitious, by noblemen requiring more spacious castles for themselves, by rulers embarking on war expeditions, by the developing manufacturing industries, and even by the religious communities as they set out to build their magnificent cathedrals. Yet Church teaching adamantly refused to condone the process without which these needs could not be satisfied. The result was that the teaching of the Church was flouted, and that capitalism flourished in defiance of clerical opposition. The pattern was set by Jewish refugees, entering Western Europe as a result of persecution by militant Islamic societies in North Africa and the Iberian peninsula. Being prevented from engaging in industrial and commercial activity in the West by the hostility of the guilds they turned to lending their carefully preserved treasure at interest to needy kings and lords. The treatment of these Jewish immigrants is one of the most shabby episodes in western history, as in general their capital was borrowed and exploited but not returned by their Christian debtors. But it served at least to demonstrate the need for a banking service in Western Europe, and where the Jewish example led the way others were prepared to follow. Bankers set up business in all the most populous centres of Europe, with the encouragement and protection of local rulers, and made possible the gradual transformation of the small-scale pattern of medieval town life and the craft guilds. The fact that this transformation took place despite the anti-usury laws of the Church only served to weaken the moral authority of the Church.

The Medieval Achievement

The unity of medieval Christendom was always more of an aspiration than a reality, but with the rise of capitalism and new independent states even the aspiration was undermined and ceased to have much significance for Western Civilisation. Capitalism and the new states were natural allies. The businessmen and bankers lent their money most readily to the stronger rulers, who were thereby enabled to become still stronger. The rulers, on their side, were anxious to promote the businessmen in the service of the state, because the new 'middle class'[3] which they represented provided a reliable ally with which to counterbalance the old aristocracy of lords and barons who yearned for the greater freedom to go their own ways which they had enjoyed (or imagined their ancestors to have enjoyed) in feudal society. This alliance with the middle class had the further advantage for the rulers that it enabled them to be more independent of the Church, because it provided a supply of lay clerics who were able to perform the administrative functions of the state which had hitherto relied heavily upon the Church for suitable personnel. The new lay clerks were more malleable to the wishes of the rulers precisely because they were more dependent upon them than was the Church.

Another feature of the alliance between the temporal rulers and the middle class was that it emphasised the civic origin of the new states. These states of Western Europe only slowly acquired precise territorial definition. They began as city-states. The importance of

London, for example, to the England of Henry II, and of Paris to the nascent France of Philip Augustus, can scarcely be exaggerated. In a real sense of wealth and power these cities *were* the states, in the same way that Venice and Genoa, Bruges and Antwerp, were independent states. The hinterland of the cities was of only peripheral importance, but as the states prospered the possession of such 'development areas' gave states such as France and England a decisive advantage over the single-city states. In any case, the ruler who had a firm base in one of the flourishing cities was well placed to co-operate with the rising middle-class families and to use their wealth in order to increase his territorial power. This happened in both France and England, as well as elsewhere in Europe, although the process was not a steady one because of wars and internecine strife, visitations of the plague and dynastic weaknesses. But by the end of the fifteenth century, the alliance of strong rulers, flourishing towns, and the capitalist middle class, had achieved its greatest success – the creation of the nation state.

The institutions which were devised to perform the essential functions of these medieval states can also be regarded as significant achievements, and in many instances their survival down to the present day demonstrates the remarkable institutional continuity within Western Civilisation over the greater part of a millennium. In England, for example, forms of common law deriving from Saxon times remain important and have made English law less responsive to the organising principles of Roman law than has been the case in other parts of Western Europe. In England, also, the Magna Carta of the thirteenth century established principles of the relationship between a ruler and his people which have subsequently provided a model and precedent even when, as in the constitutional conflict of the seventeenth century, they were misrepresented. And by the end of the thirteenth century, the organs of conciliar government, whereby the king ruled through an elaborate assembly of councils, was consummated by the development of parliament containing representatives of the three estates: aristocracy and Church in the House of Lords and commoners in the House of Commons. Through the survival of such institutions, the achievements of the medieval centuries continue to exert a profound influence on Western Civilisation today.

Perhaps even more important have been the intellectual and artistic achievements of the Middle Ages. In order to understand the scale of medieval intellectual attainments it is necessary to recall the nature of the cultural vacuum which persisted in Western Europe until the end of the eleventh century. The 'chrysalis' function of the Church in preserving classical texts and an institutional link with Hellenic Civilisation has already been noted, and there can be no doubt about the value of this service in providing a foundation for subsequent development. But this cultural legacy, for all its importance, was quantitatively slight, and there were many gaps in it. For example, the Roman authors had survived better than the Greek, the Greek texts were usually available only in Latin translations, and some Greek masterpieces such as the works of Aristotle were unknown except for a few fragments. The Church Fathers of the first few centuries AD bulked largest in the libraries of the monasteries and cathedrals, and their references to otherwise missing texts were often tantalising and frustrating. The literary legacy of the ancient world thus did little more than whet the intellectual appetite once cultural and creative activity became vigorous in the new Western Civilisation, and the first task to which several generations of medieval scholars applied themselves with persistence and remarkable success was the recovery of the corpus of Classical knowledge. Of course, complete recovery was impossible, but by diligent investigation of the sources within Western Europe, supplemented by contacts with Islamic libraries in the Iberian peninsula and elsewhere, and with the great collections in Byzantium, a vast amount of Classical literature was restored to the experience of Western Civilisation. In particular, the works of Aristotle were brought back into scholarly circulation, stirring the imagination and admiration of men who found their intellectual horizons expanding with startling rapidity.

The physical recovery of the ancient learning was thus a medieval accomplishment of considerable significance. The assimilation of this experience was a further achievement. In the twelfth century, when the impact of the recovery became widespread, the first result was an efflorescence of exuberant intellectual activity, much of it of a speculative nature such as that of Peter Abelard, with its adoption of a Socratic pattern of free dialogue. Once the initial shock wave of this seismic disturbance had been registered, however, the profoundly pietistic element in Western European Christendom reasserted itself and the problem confronting scholars became one of reconciling the ancient learning with the accepted teaching of the Christian Church. This problem was solved in monumental fashion by St Thomas

Aquinas, working in Paris a hundred years after Abelard had taught there. By skilfully integrating the intellectual system of Aristotle with Christian teaching around the central concept of Natural Law, St Thomas created a philosophical matrix which, as 'Thomism', has served as a basis for Catholic Christendom ever since. It is not too much to claim that current Catholic ideas on birth control and other matters of contemporary concern are largely conditioned by this outstanding feat of intellectual assimilation and synthesis in the thirteenth century.[4]

It should not be inferred that this achievement marked the conclusion of medieval intellectual accomplishments. Like academics at all times, the medieval schoolmen – the scholars in the various seats of learning – were exceedingly contentious people. Later generations have been inclined to mock the supposed abstract triviality of the subjects about which they argued, like the celebrated problem of how many angels can dance upon the point of a needle. But when it is remembered that angels are incorporeal beings and that the point of a needle represents zero, the problem can be recast in terms of spatial relationships which present a genuine philosophical problem. The medieval mind flexed its intellectual muscles on such problems, and conflicting interpretations developed into rival groups of scholars. Amongst these, some pioneered the way for subsequent developments in science and philosophy. The revolutionary hypothesis of Copernicus in 1543, that the sun and not the earth is the centre of the universe, can be interpreted as an application of 'Occam's Razor', the principle enunciated by the fourteenth-century English philosopher William of Occam that beings should not be multiplied without necessity – that is, a simple solution is always to be preferred to a complicated one if they make equal sense of the available data. This was but one of many instances in which medieval scholars prepared the way for and even anticipated later intellectual innovations.

One great restraint upon the medieval intellect, however, was the strong sense of the authority of the ancient masters. This derived partly from the habit of mind within Christendom, where the authority of the New Testament texts, as annotated and interpreted by the early Church Fathers, was accepted as beyond dispute. But it also stemmed from the circumstances in which the works of Classical scholarship had been recovered, and from the respectful and almost reverential way in which these new texts were assimilated into

European culture. It meant that the world views of Aristotle and Ptolemy, the medical wisdom of Galen, and the mathematical principles of Pythagoras and Euclid, were accepted as part of the authoritative bed-rock of human experience, and this attitude was inimical to the growth of a critical scientific spirit. The abandonment of this restraint was probably the single most important aspect of the scientific revolution of the sixteenth and seventeenth centuries. Nevertheless, as with any manifestation of maturity, the abandonment of traditional authorities could only come with confidence gained from a thorough understanding of these authorities, and it was such an understanding that was made possible by the very significant achievements of the medieval intellect.

Medieval creativity was less impeded by the bonds of authoritarianism in its practical aspects than in the realm of the intellect. In works of art, in technology, and even in experimental science, the Middle Ages in Europe demonstrated a remarkable innovative vitality which constitutes a set of long-lasting and important achievements. The most splendid of medieval works of art were the great Gothic cathedrals of Europe, with their adventurous design involving new techniques in masonry construction, and their embellishment giving unprecedented scope to the craftsmen in stained glass and other arts.[5] Amongst technological innovations, the centuries of medieval expansion witnessed the vigorous exploitation of water power, pioneered the use of wind power in windmills and greatly advanced the sophistication of the sailing ship, and invented new types of mechanism which, beginning with the mechanical clock, went on to apply the ingenious devices of gears, cranks, springs, and regulators to other forms of machine.[6] Experimental science, also, although still in its infancy, was not without achievements. The alchemical search for the 'philosopher's stone' was unsuccessful, but promoted significant developments in metallurgy, just as the search for perpetual motion stimulated work on clockwork mechanisms and promoted investigation into the principles of dynamics. And the investigations of the famous experimenter Friar Roger Bacon, the Franciscan scientist of the thirteenth century, resulted in the invention of gunpowder, which must be reckoned amongst the most potent innovations of Western Civilisation.

Far from being the wilderness of prescientific superstition that they were until quite recently thought to be, the 500 years from AD 1000, in which Western Civilisation became conscious of its identity and began to expand, were years of very considerable intellectual achievements. The expansion, to be sure, was internal rather than external. There was little change in the territorial frontiers of Western Europe from the tenth to the fifteenth centuries, except for the Christian conquest of the Iberian peninsula. In this respect, the sequence of crusading expeditions to the eastern Mediterranean and Holy Land brought no permanent gains, although they were not without important effects in stimulating trade and intellectual exchanges. But internally, there was a quite extraordinary outburst of expansive activity, in the growth of towns, trade, and strong new states, and in the various intellectual and practical activities which we have considered. In one institution, in particular, this period produced an administrative innovation which was to become one of the most distinctive features of the period and a unique agent of intellectual progress. This was the university.[7] Assemblies of scholars had existed before in the ancient world, usually gathered around some great teacher, and others existed at that time in the courts of some of the Islamic rulers. But the striking feature of the medieval universities was that they were self-governing, self-perpetuating bodies of scholars, both teachers and students. They seemed to spring spontaneously from cathedral schools and similar ecclesiastical institutions of instruction, responding to the need of new governments for clerical underpinning, and thriving on the intense intellectual excitement of the twelfth century when the lost masterpieces of the Classical Age were being recovered. There seems to have been a considerable traffic of poor students around Europe, wandering from one school to another, studying medicine at Salerno, law at Bologna, and theology at Paris. As these schools asserted their independence, either as 'colleges' of students as at Bologna or as courses of study provided by recognised teachers as in Paris, they acquired the corporate character which has remained ever since the distinguishing characteristic of the university.

As in other aspects of medieval life, the pietistic and authoritarian assumptions of Christendom remained strong, so that the curriculum defined in the medieval universities placed great emphasis on the training of clerks for Holy Orders, but the 'seven liberal arts' which became the staple undergraduate fare of the universities allowed plenty of scope for the expression of other talents. The corporate assemblies of the universities normally acquired charters from the appropriate temporal or ecclesiastical rulers and, once set up, have continued to exist ever since. By receiving endowments of property they acquired material foundations and, even more important, by their continued service to the society of their times, they have earned the recognition of governments even when they have retained their independence. There were six European universities by the end of the twelfth century, and by 1500 this number had risen to seventy-six. Thus the university had established itself as a major contribution of the medieval centuries to Western Civilisation.

5. The Mainspring of European Growth

The Europe which emerged from the period of medieval consolidation was in many respects recognisable as the Europe of today. Distinct linguistic traditions provided fertile ground for the development of nationalism, and many political, legal, and academic institutions had been created which have enjoyed a continuous existence from the Middle Ages to the present. But in other ways the differences between Europe in the early sixteenth century and the twentieth century are more significant than the similarities. In particular, Western European Civilisation in 1500 occupied a modest backwater of world politics, whereas 400 years later it had come to wield an absolute world ascendancy. This transformation was the result of profound changes within Western Civilisation, which will be explored in this and subsequent chapters. At the outset, however, it is important to stress both the continuity and the dynamism of the process which make it possible to relate a succession of disruptive innovations, both material and intellectual, to a stable core of European institutions. Thus it is possible to maintain that, despite all the changes which have characterised Western Civilisation over the last five centuries, it is still essentially a continuation of the civilisation which had established itself in Western Europe during the previous half-millennium.

Renaissance, Reformation and Nation States

The European Renaissance of the fifteenth and sixteenth centuries has received a lot of attention from historians, so that a popular convention has arisen of regarding it as the signal of the transition from the Middle Ages to the period of Modern Europe. According to this conventional view, the Renaissance began in Italy in the fifteenth century (or even in the thirteenth or fourteenth century, if it is desired to include Dante as a harbinger of the movement). It was distinguished, firstly, by a rejection of the arid scholasticism of medieval divines in favour of the illumination of Classical art, architecture, and literature; secondly, by a far-reaching attempt to adopt these works of Classical Greece and Rome as models for refashioning art and life; and thirdly, by an extraordinary flowering of artistic creativity which went beyond the models of antiquity, by developing new principles such as that of perspective in painting.

It can hardly be denied that there is some content to this view, even when it is reproduced in such a crude summary as given here. The Italian city-states of the late Middle Ages were the scene of great political rivalries and of commercial and intellectual vitality. They were jealous of their independence both from each other and from the interference of outside potentates, including the Pope and Emperor. The laborious rediscovery by medieval scholars of the works of Classical antiquity had placed at the disposal of the citizens of these small Italian states visions of grandeur achieved by their ancestors and alternative, largely secularised, models of citizenship which were different from those of medieval Christendom. At the same time, the commercial success of cities such as Venice and Genoa in capturing the bulk of the Mediterranean trade and much of that with northern Europe, ensured that a steady flow of wealth came to Italy and enriched those social classes who were most enthusiastic about classical models and who had the leisure to embellish their property with works of art and to give their patronage to artists and craftsmen. Such economic and social considerations, of course, do not *explain* aesthetic creativity, but they demonstrate the existence of an environment which was highly congenial to it. In this situation, men of ability and even of genius in the arts have scope to flourish and to be recognised, and so it was in fifteenth-century Italy.

But the mood passed, and so did the socio-economic preconditions. Like the city-states of Classical Greece, those of Italy squandered much of their wealth and resources on internecine rivalries which left most of them in subjection to one or other of the great external powers that had been drawn into the country by the prospect of territorial aggrandisement. Their commercial prosperity passed steadily and irreversibly to the maritime nations of Western Europe which were able to take better advantage of the opportunities for trade opened up by the voyages of exploration. And perhaps most influential of all the factors in the eclipse of the Italian Renaissance, the renewed Catholic militancy of the Counter-Reformation had its headquarters in Rome, and the neighbouring states and provinces of the Italian peninsula felt the full force of the repressive intellectual influence of such institutions as the Inquisition. Under the new political and religious régimes of the sixteenth century, therefore, the vast spate of artistic creativity which had been the most sensational feature of the Italian Renaissance was reduced to a trickle, and the leadership of Europe in both politics and art moved northwards and westwards. It did not disappear completely. The stimulus given to the scientific revolution by the work of Galileo in the first half of the seventeenth century bears witness to the survival of high intellectual performance in Italy. But the fate of Galileo at the hands of the papal Holy Office shows the difficulties confronting any such achievement, and it is significant that the next steps in the advance of science were taken north of the Alps, by Bacon, Descartes, and Newton.

The concept of 'renaissance' involves a sense of rebirth, of the coming again of elements of a lost golden age fom the past. In such a sense historians have identified a succession of European events as renaissances, beginning with the Carolingian Renaissance of the ninth century and going on through the twelfth-century Renaissance to that of Italy in the fifteenth century. In every case the inspiration to intellectual activity has been the rediscovery of ancient works and ideas – usually those of Classical Greece and Rome. In every case, moreover, there has been a fusion between the Classical ideas and those of the contemporary culture into which they have been reborn, and it is this blending of old and new which has given singularity to each renaissance and to the works of artistic and intellectual creativity characterising it. This combination of past and present was most marked in the Italian Renaissance of the fifteenth century. For one thing, the knowledge of Classical Rome was fuller than it had been previously, and the desire to emulate Roman achievements was associated with the first stirrings of an Italian nationalism. Yet Italy in this period also possessed a self-confidence which made it less dependent on past custom and practice than any society for over a millennium. In some sense men began to feel that the Golden Age had been surpassed, and to look to the future with an expectancy of even greater achievements which was in itself a new feature in European thinking. The Italian Renaissance, in short, boosted the hopes of men and encouraged the development of an idea of progress.

Progress, when it came, did not come in the way anticipated. In the first place, the artistic creativity by which the Italian Renaissance is chiefly remembered, faded away to be replaced by different sorts of aesthetic expression in Germany, France, England, and Spain. These diverse forms of intellectual activity were less 'renaissances' than the Italian experience because they derived more from a discovery of innate linguistic or national characteristics than from a recovery of a lost cultural tradition. The brilliant intellectual efflorescence of Elizabethan England, for example, although not without inspiration from other European sources, was essentially the expression of a new-found nationalism. This was something new rather than a rebirth. It was also a development which was not anticipated until it actually occurred. This was also the case with another convention-shattering innovation of the sixteenth century: the division of Christendom by the Protestant Reformation.

The Reformation has frequently been linked with the Renaissance as the other agent in a double transformation by which Western Civilisation passed from the Middle Ages to modern times. The two events had common features. As Renaissance men looked back to Classical Rome for their inspiration, so Protestantism looked back to the early Church and argued that the accretions of fifteen centuries of institutional Christianity were dispensable. The motive for the restoration of 'primitive' Christianity by the Protestants was a profound dissatisfaction with late-medieval Christendom, which had become institutionally moribund when it was not actually corrupt. It was concerned more with the recovery of spirituality than with the restoration of any particular form of Church government, but its critique inevitably assumed an institutional form and it rapidly threw up new institutions of its own. Ironically, much of the initial stimulus for Protestantism came from Renaissance humanists such as Erasmus and More, who applied their Classical scholarship to a searching criticism of the spiritual deficiencies of contemporary Christendom, but then refused to join the attack on the Catholic Church.

This refusal marked a divergence between the Renaissance and the Reformation. Instead of men of Classical culture and broad humanity, the leadership of the Reformation and the Counter-Reformation which it generated within the Catholic Church passed to men of intense but obsessive spirituality who were frequently bigots and never tolerant of religious views differing from their own. The result was a disaster for Western Civilisation, with a century of crippling religious wars and a legacy of contempt and intolerance which has not yet been entirely dissipated in the second half of the twentieth century. Of course, there have been mitigating features in this disaster, amongst which the noble individualism of Martin Luther's commitment: 'Here I stand, I can no other', and the dedicated spirituality of men such as Ignatius Loyola and George Fox, are significant examples, and it may be argued that the tradition of European liberalism owes much to the forging and testing which it received in the religious conflicts following the Reformation. On balance, however, it is hard to avoid the conclusion that the losses have far outweighed the gains in this conflict, and that the conflict has been a painful atavism which has warped the development of Western Civilisation in ways which have been profoundly important. Outstanding amongst these distortions has been the rise of nation states and the loss of such international consciousness as was provided by the medieval conception of Christendom.

The Reformation owed its endurance as a movement to the new nation states of northern Europe. There had been protests against the worldliness of the Church long before Martin Luther. Some of these, like the Cathars and Albigensians of southern France, had been cruelly exterminated. Others like the personal crusade of Francis of Assissi, had been shrewdly incorporated within the church by a perceptive Pope. Others again, like the protests of Wycliffe and Hus, had been allowed some freedom of expression before they were crushed. It was the misfortune of Western Civilisation that the attempt was made to crush the Reformation rather than to incorporate it as a radical movement within Christendom. Once this decision had been taken, it is most improbable that Martin Luther or those who followed him could have survived without the protection of the new nation states of Europe. Luther himself was adopted by the Elector of Saxony, a German ruler proud of the independence of his state, who saw in the Reformation an opportunity to assert this independence against the external claims of the Emperor and the Pope. Within a few years, the religious protest movement took root in other German states, in Switzerland, and England, for very similar reasons. For Henry VIII of England, the Reformation provided a pretext for the solution of his marital and political problems, although so far as religion was concerned he preserved the title of

THE MAINSPRING OF EUROPEAN GROWTH

'Defender of the Faith' conferred by a grateful papacy for his attack on Luther. The English Reformation was thus more of a political than a religious event, the justification of the claim in the preamble to the Act in Restraint of Appeals in 1533, that 'this realm of England is an empire' even though that empire stretched no further than Calais and Dublin.

The fact that the Protestant Reformation was accepted for political reasons by the nation states of northern Europe does not imply that there were less effective nation states elsewhere in Europe. On the contrary, the strong new states of southern Europe included France and Spain, both of which reached their own agreement or 'concordat' with the papacy whereby the powers of the Catholic Church were permanently curtailed in relation to those of the secular state. Thus the emergence of nation states represented a step towards state control of religion and ultimately towards complete secularisation of political power in both Protestant and Catholic parts of the now-divided Christendom. There are some grounds for thinking that it is over-stretching the term to refer to these new states as 'nation states'. As we have noted in the previous chapter, most of these states sprang from strong dynastic bases in the increasingly wealthy commercial and industrial towns of Europe. A few of them, such as Spain, were the result of dynastic alliances combined with military conquest when the Iberian peninsula was recovered from Islamic settlement. Some of them, like the German states, retained a loose affiliation to a larger association – in this case, the vestigial remains of the Holy Roman Empire. But the more typical cases, and ultimately the more significant, were those such as France and England, where a skilful dynasty established stronger institutions of central government than any known before, and used the resulting power base as a means of pursuing aggressively independent policies. Only in a secondary sense could these states be regarded as nations. Certainly, both French and English nationalism had been stirred by the Hundred Years' War, and distinct linguistic traditions were developing rapidly, but it is probably being anachronistic (like Shakespeare in his Chronicle Plays) to attribute a strong sense of patriotism to any period before the sixteenth century, because loyalties tended to be either more general (to Church and Christendom), or more particular (to province and dynasty), than they became under the influence of nationalism. Given the growth of strong states, however, the split in Christendom and the consequent descent into international chaos spiced with acute religious rivalry did much to promote a sense of isolation, independence, and nationalism, so that by the end of the sixteenth century the scenario of modern European politics, with its conflicting nation states all fiercely jealous of their sovereignty, was well established.

Here, again, the period around the beginning of the sixteenth century can be seen as a turning-point in Western Civilisation. Like the two-faced deity Janus of Classical mythology, it was a period which looked both to the past and the future. Western man had hitherto regarded the Golden Age as lying in the past: in the glories of Greece and Rome, and in the days of the founder of Christianity and the Early Fathers of the Church. Both these images provided inspiration to the period we are considering, through the Renaissance and Reformation. But unlike corresponding movements in the Middle Ages, the Renaissance and Reformation also turned men's thoughts to the future: to the prospect of unfolding vistas of achievement, in the discovery of new continents, the founding of new empires, and in accepting novel intellectual challenges. This Janus-posture of maintaining continuity with institutions already established, while striking out into uncharted intellectual territory, is the most intriguing aspect of the period. It was, however, an unequal balance, as the attraction of the future proved to be stronger than that of the past. In two particular respects the experience of novelty proved overwhelming: the impact of the new geographical explorations, and the intellectual revolution associated with modern science.

The Expansion of Europe

The expansion of Western Civilisation from Europe to influence all other parts of the world is one of the most remarkable events of human history, having an enduring significance at political, commercial, social and cultural levels. It was also an adventure story of heroic proportions and breath-taking achievements, so that it captured the imagination of western man and filled his mind with new images. The process began tentatively, with the various attempts by German emperors and princes to establish settlements in the Slav-occupied territories east of the Elbe, and with the missions of the crusaders to recover the Holy Land from the possession of the infidel.

These early expansive movements had little more than a local influence, and in the case of the crusades failed completely to fulfil their objective, although they did help to set a pattern for subsequent expansion by showing the prospects for trade and for satisfying the land-hunger of aristocratic families. Thus the success of Venice in establishing a commercial empire in the eastern Mediterranean in the wake of the crusaders, and the settlement of militant Norman noblemen in the Holy Land, were instructive precursors of processes which occurred on a much larger scale after 1500.

The 'modern' wave of expansion began in the middle of the fifteenth century, with the Portuguese voyages of exploration southwards along the coast of Africa. The Portuguese mariners eventually turned the Cape of Good Hope and penetrated into the Indian Ocean, rapidly establishing a vast trading empire in India and the East Indies. Meanwhile, the newly united states of Spain had sponsored the exploits of the Genoese adventurer Christopher Columbus, who in 1492 made the first of his three voyages to discover a shorter route to the Indies by sailing west rather than east. Although he died believing that this is what he had achieved, the Spanish explorers who flooded in his wake soon realised that what he had discovered was in fact a huge new continent, and that beyond this lay a further ocean before the Indies could be reached. Within thirty years of Columbus' first voyage, Magellan's expedition had successfully circumnavigated the earth and Spanish domination had been established in the Caribbean islands and in Mexico. It was shortly thereafter extended into South America. By vanquishing the Aztecs of Mexico and the Incas of Peru the Spanish 'conquistadores' annexed complete empires with unbelievable wealth in bullion available to replenish the coffers of the government back in Europe. And to seal the great accomplishments of Portugal and Spain the Pope had conveniently divided the terrestrial globe between the two, to prevent conflict and to ensure the spread of the Christian gospel to the new-discovered heathen.

Had Western Europe been enjoying a period of relative stability, it is possible that this attempt to carve up the discoveries equitably between the main participants would have been generally accepted. But it was not, and the expansion of European influence became inextricably involved in the new tensions of the Protestant Reformation and militant nationalism. By the second half of the sixteenth century, England and France were becoming involved in the expansive movement, and they were soon joined by the newly liberated Netherlands. They began as pirates, preying on the widely scattered trading stations and treasure fleets of Spain and Portugal. But they quickly moved on to the stage of setting up trading stations and settlements of their own, so that the world became laced with a novel network of trading relationships as rival European interests competed with each other to exploit the commercial possibilities of the newly accessible territories. All the early settlements were on islands or on the continental coasts, because the oceans were the great highways of the sea-borne empires which flourished in this period. In some thickly populated parts of the world such as the East Indies, the imperial trading stations, first of the Portuguese and then of the Dutch, remained on the coasts because there was never any serious European attempt to establish homes in these colonies, and because the power of the European rulers diminished rapidly away from the coasts. These could be kept under supervision by the superior ships and fire-power of European technology, but inland the small European forces were vulnerable to the superior numbers of the existing inhabitants. Only in India, under British rule, was a successful attempt made to press European authority into the hinterland, and in this case it was achieved by taking advantage of rivalries between Indian princes.[1]

A very different relationship with the native inhabitants was established in those new territories which were either thinly pop-ulated or which could be brought effectively under European control. This was the situation in most of the American territories, so that it was in the islands and coastal regions of this enormous land mass that the most effective and permanent settlements were created. The first settlers hoped for quick riches in the form of gold and silver, and for a brief generation the Spanish dream of El Dorado, the city of gold, was amply fulfilled. But then the bullion had to be won by more laborious means, including complex mining operations, and later settlers turned their attention to producing commodities which would sell in European markets, so that plan-tations to cultivate sugar were created in the Caribbean islands and the plantation economy was then adapted for the production of tobacco and cotton. Essential to this economy was a substantial labour force, and when it became apparent that native American labour was not adequate for this purpose the plantation colonists turned to the purchase of negro slaves from Africa. Thus was reintroduced into the western tradition an institution which had lapsed to all practical effect with the Roman Empie. It may well be regarded as morally one of the most deplorable episodes in the history of modern Europe, but as a demographic factor the removal of a large negro population across the Atlantic has had incalculable repercussions on the course of American development.

Other factors as well as greed and commerce figured amongst the motives of the colonists who moved out of Europe in this great wave of expansion. Some settlements, in America and later in Australia, were penal colonies, and their first 'citizens' were the convicts and the prison officers. More significant were the colonies of religious refugees. The Pilgrim Fathers sailed from Plymouth in the *Mayflower* in 1620 and founded the first of the New England colonies. They had been persecuted for their puritanism at home, but in America their religious commitment helped them to survive the formidable problems which beset the settlement in its early years and they eventually became a haven for other religious dissidents from the mother country. Later still, William Penn established the important Quaker colony named after him, and Maryland was settled initially by Roman Catholic refugees. These seaboard colonies of permanent settlement marked the beginning of a very significant ethnic migration of white races across the Atlantic, and provided a springboard from which the vast interior of the continent could eventually be opened up and settled.

Meanwhile, European rivalries were constantly being projected in colonial conflict. The Portuguese lost most of their East Indian empire to the Dutch in the seventeenth century, and in the following century Britain annexed most of the settlements of Holland and France in North America. The European powers fought continuously for possession of the West Indian islands, which were particularly prized for their sugar production, but Spain maintained its grip upon the mainland colonies around the Caribbean and in South America until the wars of liberation at the beginning of the nineteenth century. By that time long-settled colonies had a useful precedent for successful rebellion in the experience of the original thirteen British colonies, which had decided to go their own way in 1776 and demonstrated their military ability to ensure that they did so. The American War of Independence promoted fresh thinking about the policy of imperial expansion and the role of colonies. By a singular coincidence, 1776 was also the year of publication of Adam

Smith's treatise on *The Wealth of Nations* which for the first time set the study of economic relationships on a systematic basis and revealed the inadequacies of previous commercial policies. Smith condemned these policies under the general title of 'mercantilism'. His judgement was unnecessarily severe, because the policies which he attacked did not represent a single coherent point of view but were rather a rag-bag collection of precepts, precedents, and rule-of-thumb common sense acquired from three centuries of dealing with the novel situation of European expansion. They were the gestation process of modern economic theory, and should not be judged too harshly when they conflict retrospectively with the formulations of the economists of later generations.[2]

Essentially, mercantilism was an attempt to wrestle with the problems of the expanding world trade which followed the voyages of discovery and the subsequent wave of conquest and colonisation. The context of European national rivalries of the period ensured that this problem was examined in relation to the interests of the nation states. Mercantilism can thus be interpreted as a policy aimed at exploiting the new sources of wealth through trade for the benefit of the mother-country of the policy-maker. In the first stage of its development it took the form of a crude 'bullionism', expressed in the belief that the primary objective of trade and colonies was to ensure a flow of gold and silver to the mother-country. The experience of Spain, however, provided a useful object lesson in the weaknesses of this policy, because Spain was spectacularly afflicted in the sixteenth and seventeenth centuries by its dependence on an apparently limitless inflow of bullion. In the first place, domestic industries were neglected, so that the country had to pay for the import of manufactured commodities and services. Secondly, the impact of the American bullion on the monetary systems of Europe was disastrous, as it caused a general devaluation of the coinages and became a diminishing asset. And finally, the limitless inflow of bullion was shown to be an illusion, and when it did begin to dwindle it left Spain an impoverished third-rate power.

Reflecting on this experience, the more perceptive statesmen of Europe realised that it was more important for national strength to ensure self-sufficiency than to rely on bullion to purchase the produce of others. Thus, in the second half of the seventeenth century, Louis XIV's minister Colbert recognised the value of encouraging French industries by offering subsidies to craftsmen and protecting them

from foreign competition. The active middle-class mercantile communities of England and Holland went a step further, to demonstrate
that neither dependence on bullion nor national self-sufficiency were
as important as generating a cumulative trading relationship whereby national manufactured commodities were exported in order to
obtain foreign goods and raw materials for domestic industrial
processes. The manifest success of this policy in cities such as London
and Amsterdam prepared the ground for the formulation of
economic theory by Adam Smith. It also promoted the development
of financial institutions such as banks and stock exchanges with a
much more sophisticated understanding of the nature of money than
that which had existed before, and it provided powerful support for
the economic stimulation of colonies to produce such goods as would
be most welcome in the mother-country. Unfortunately for the later
mercantilists, they persisted in maintaining the mother-country-
colony relationship, and it was this persistence which led to the
collapse of the so-called 'old colonial system' in 1776, at the hands of
the American colonists and Adam Smith.

In *The Wealth of Nations* Adam Smith succeeded in showing that,
given the minimum of state encouragement and protection, the self-
interest of industrialists, merchants, bankers, and so on, would be
sufficient to promote trading relationships from which all parties
stood to benefit. He demonstrated for the first time, moreover, the
mechanics of the whole process of wealth-creation, from the
importance of specialisation in the processes of production to the
exchange of credit between financial institutions. As parts of this
process he focused attention on labour and capital, and initiated a
controversy which has continued ever since about the respective
roles of these factors of production. The fact that much of this
controversy has been misconceived, and in the last century has been
grossly over-simplified into a conflict between 'capitalist' and
'socialist' modes of production, merely serves to show the importance of Smith's analysis. What is involved is our understanding of
the whole process of wealth-creation, and Smith was surely correct in
showing this to be an intricate process involving *both* capital and
labour. We have already recognised the importance of wealth-
creation in the formation of civilisations, and the basic techniques
were familiar in the ancient world. Medieval Europe, however, had
stumbled upon a process of *continuing* wealth-creation, by transforming savings into investments and by relating them to industry

and commerce. In this way, the generation of wealth became cumulative, and avoided the trap of stagnation, over-taxation and decay into which the Roman economic system had fallen. The process had been expanded, refined, and institutionalised, before Smith provided it with a theoretical justification. It deserves to be regarded as one of the most significant discoveries of Western Civilisation. In a practical sense, it was the mainspring of European growth, if we may beg for the moment the question of how the mainspring is coiled. The expansion of Europe was both promoted by the process of continuing wealth-creation, and served greatly to magnify the scale and success of this process.

The Intellectual Revolution

As if the upheavals of the Renaissance, the Reformation, the rise of nation states, and the explosive expansion of European influence, were not enough to justify the view that Western Civilisation underwent a significant reorientation around the beginning of the sixteenth century, there was another transformation of even greater profundity which began to occur about the same time. This was a revolution in the intellectual framework within which western man thought and reasoned. It has been represented as similar to the physical process of standing everybody on their heads, so important was the shift in consciousness.[3] Men looked at the world with new eyes, seeing things in ways they had never been seen before – and no longer seeing them according to the traditional point of view. Of course, the Renaissance and the religious wars, the need to justify support for one's nation state, and the mind-boggling effects of the voyages of discovery and the expansion of Europe, all contributed to this intellectual revolution. But the total effect was greater than the sum of these parts. A wholly new consciousness emerged, and it is this which requires examination.

To a considerable extent, the intellectual revolution of the sixteenth and seventeenth centuries, was associated with the origin of modern science. It is as well to be clear, as we approach this concept, what we mean by it, and it should be observed immediately that 'science' has greatly narrowed its meaning in the last two hundred years. Up to the nineteenth century, it could be used to designate any field of study or search for knowledge, so that there was no difficulty about including history within its scope, or even of claiming that theology was 'the queen of the sciences'. Only comparatively recently has the term been limited to certain areas of the natural world, and largely to physical phenomena. It is probably inevitable that, in pursuit of increasing specialisation in the search for knowledge as in other things, this should have happened, but it should warn us that in its emergence at the beginning of modern European history science had wider implications than would be apparent from the contemporary narrow use of the term.

Modern science emerged from the swaddling clothes of medieval science, which was in turn an immensely ingenious recreation of ancient science, and in particular the world view of Aristotle with practical additions provided by the medicine of Galen and the model of an earth-centred universe controlled by intricate geometrical relationships laid down by Ptolemy. This world view had the authority of antiquity behind it, together with the authority it acquired by the successful assimilation of Aristotelianism with Christianity. The universe of Aristotle thus had come to be the universe of Christendom, and to challenge one was to challenge both. Despite the formidable authority of this orthodoxy, some aspects had already come under critical review in the Middle Ages. For one thing, increasing familiarity with the ancient masters showed that they did not all agree with Aristotle, so that alternative world-views could show an ancestry as distinguished as his. Again, on examination, anomalies were found in the orthodox doctrine, as when anatomical dissections demonstrated inaccuracies in Galen's text. Then, the sudden increments to European knowledge which followed the voyages of discovery had to be accommodated, and these placed an increasing strain on the established orthodoxies. The more relaxed intellectual environment of Renaissance humanism gave an opportunity for heterodox views to be canvassed, and the new technological medium of the printing press permitted a wider dispersal of new ideas than had been possible before. The stage was thus set for an intellectual revolution which would topple Aristotle from his throne. But it was far from clear what would take his place.

In the event, the throne was left vacant. No single authority could be permitted to assert the sort of intellectual hegemony that had been allowed Aristotle. For what was unseated was not just the authority of Aristotle, but authority itself. Never again, in the mainstream of the western intellectual tradition, could any authority be accepted without question. This dethroning of authority is at the core of the intellectual revolution. In a sense, this revolution is both a personal and a collective pilgrimage. Every individual has to make it for himself or herself, because we all begin life in dependence upon the beliefs and opinions of others, and we all come to the point of maturity where we have the opportunity of taking responsibility for our own beliefs. But this is only possible because of the collective pilgrimage of Western Civilisation, in which the opportunity for individual responsibility has come to be regarded as an essential intellectual birth-right. In other cultures this opportunity would have been – and still is – regarded as intolerable. Such has been the scale of the intellectual revolution.

It could be argued that science itself now occupies the throne vacated by Aristotelian orthodoxy, and that the scientific method guarantees the opportunity for individual responsibility. There are, however, serious difficulties about accepting this point of view. The first is the difficulty about the constricted meaning that 'science' has acquired, which would imply giving more significance to the natural and physical sciences today than they intellectually deserve. The second is the confusion that persists about the 'scientific method', which would be compounded by the elevation of science to the role of authoritative orthodoxy. The trouble here is that there is a series of scientific methods, all of which may be appropriate to a particular search for knowledge. The primary scientific method is that of collecting evidence and arranging it systematically, in a way which has varied little from the early Sumerian observation of the heavenly bodies to Charles Darwin's collection of beetles. Then there is the method of applying deductive reasoning to the field under examination, deriving conclusions from logical or mathematical arguments which relate the observed phenomena in a comprehensive interpretation. This method has been used in the search for knowledge from Pythagoras through Descartes to modern theoretical physics. Thirdly, the inductive reasoning of the experimental method has achieved very substantial results in modern science, from Galileo's practical (and repeatable) observations to modern experimental studies in pharmaceutics and microbiology. So successful has this method been that it has been claimed for it that it is *the* scientific method of modern science. But this claim cannot be sustained, because the other methods remain important. Fourthly, there is the method of 'applied science', which derives from the belief that science is to be used for the good of mankind. This has been an outstanding characteristic of modern science ever since Francis Bacon expounded the doctrine in the early seventeenth century, but it depends for its effectiveness on a combination of the other techniques, so once again this method should not be stressed to the neglect of the others. Given this amalgam of divergent approaches to scientific knowledge, it is unwise to seek any single authoritative method amongst them. We are on safer ground in interpreting modern science as the destroyer of orthodox authorities. Any scientific authority is vulnerable to the criticism of further research and is unlikely to endure for long.

The course of the scientific revolution is of less concern to us than its contribution to the intellectual revolution of Western Civilisation. All the same, it will be convenient to summarise its main lines. The posthumous publication, in 1543, of Nicolas Copernicus' treatise *Of the Revolution of the Heavenly Bodies*, subjected the earth-centred model of the universe to the logical test of Occam's razor and demonstrated that it greatly simplified the model to put the sun in the centre. Copernicus was probably wise to delay publication of this heterodox thesis until after his death, because it was immediately denounced by all religious persuasions, and it was not until observations with the newly invented telescope started to corroborate the heliocentric interpretation at the beginning of the seventeenth century that orthodoxy began to crumble. It was then subjected to simultaneous blows from Bacon's attacks on Aristotelian science and Galileo's experiments in physics, so that by the second half of the century the ground was prepared for a new synthesis, carried out by Isaac Newton. This showed how the whole observable universe responded to mathematical, mechanical, principles like a gigantic piece of clockwork. The image of the mechanical clock came to exercise a powerful hold on the imagination of western man.

Meanwhile, the sciences of anatomy, physiology, and medicine, were similarly throwing off their bondage to classical antiquity and were striking out on exciting new lines of enquiry, both deductive and experimental. Rather later, the study of chemistry, the underlying architecture of matter, began to develop, although it remained hampered until late in the eighteenth century, not so much by the dominance of the ancient masters as by certain misconceptions in the initial attempt to organise the matter of the natural world into categories appropriate for further examination. By the beginning of the nineteenth century, significant growth was taking place in the sciences of geology, biology, zoology, and botany. Scientific techniques had at last won general acceptance, and strong institutions had emerged to promote them. The institutionalisation of science was to lead to the limitation of the conception of science, as already suggested, but it added to the power of the studies recognised as science to pursue their enquiries, often with world-shaking consequences.

Modern science has transformed the sense of time and space of western man. In place of the cosy earth-centred universe inherited from the ancient world, with a life-span which was generally agreed could be no more than a few thousand years, modern man finds himself in an infinite universe in which the life-span of this planet alone is measured in thousands of millions of years. This alteration in scale has contributed powerfully to the intellectual revolution by which men are deprived of external authority and obliged – if they wish to assert themselves as free, responsible persons – to stand intellectually on their own feet and to define their own beliefs. For in the last resort, the intellectual revolution has been a religious revolution. Modern man has found it increasingly difficult to accept the dogma and anthropomorphic mythology of the orthodox religions. The change has been gradual and sometimes painful, frequently accompanied by a strong sense of loss. It is subsumed in the concepts of secularisation and the quest for rationality. At the beginning of the twentieth century, the eminent sociologist Max Weber sought an explanation for the growth of these distinctively modern habits of mind, and found it in the influence of Protestantism on the work ethic. He was particularly impressed by the high sense of vocation or work-motivation expressed in the lives of the extreme Protestant groups who were inspired by the teaching of John Calvin. These groups took a variety of forms, but can be conveniently linked under the English term of 'puritans', that is, those who tried to order their lives according to principles of purity and dedication. Through the influence of puritanism, Weber argued, European civilisation acquired the discipline necessary for the relentless search for rationality in the shape of modern science and intellectual organisation, and the equally relentless search for profit through business enterprise.[4]

The Weber thesis was attractive because it appeared to make sense of some of the most perplexing innovations of modern Western Civilisation, and for two generations scholars have debated its merits. Despite considerable criticism of its details, the central argument of the thesis – that there is a positive correlation between puritanism on the one hand and rationality, scientific research, and industrial expansion, on the other – still stands. But in order to survive it has been necessary to give a wider interpretation to 'puritanism' than that envisaged by Weber. Critics pointed out that all the features distinguished by Weber as characteristic of the modern world were in existence, albeit in embryo, before the Protestant Reformation, and showed the importance of Jewish bankers and Venetian merchants in the medieval economy. Other critics observed that Weber himself was distorting the meaning of puritanism by choosing as leading illustrations men so diverse as John Wesley and Benjamin Franklin. Yet by taking puritanism out of its specifically Protestant context – and even, to some extent, out of its specifically religious context – it is possible to meet both these lines of criticism. In this way, it can be argued that puritanism represents a self-disciplined approach to life characterised by a strong sense of purpose and expressed in a dedicated application to the pursuit of this purpose. Eating, drinking, and the enjoyment of leisure or relaxation, are rarely included in this purpose, so that the single-minded disregard for such subsidiary parts of life has given puritanism the qualities which have frequently made it unpopular with less dedicated individuals. Such attitudes, needless to say, long pre-date Western Civilisation: puritanism in this form was a powerful tradition in the Old Testament, and has remained typical of Jewish communities ever since. In part, this may be because it thrives as a minority attitude, as a way in which a small group preserves its distinction from a racial, national, or religious majority. Puritanism is thus seen in its starkest in the self-discipline of an *élite* group, be they Quaker businessmen, Cromwellian Roundheads, or Lenin's Bolsheviks. The last example demonstrates the possibility of a secular form of puritanism, as it shares virtually all the puritan characteristics of the other examples except the Christian theology. And in so far as we are concerned with the explanation of an intellectual revolution, the particular theological formulation may be regarded as dispensable. What is important is that puritan attitudes of discipline, application, and motivation, became dominant in a crucial period of the evolution of the modern world, and that through this dominance the progress of rationality, science, and industrial organisation became possible.

There is inevitably a certain circularity in this argument, as puritanism can be seen as the consequence of rationality as well as its cause, but in the period under consideration the novel experiences of the voyages of discovery and the rupture of Christendom created circumstances in which the puritan qualities could flourish as never before. It showed itself, moreover, not only in the earnestness of divines on both sides of the Reformation chasm, like John Calvin and Ignatius Loyola, but also in the search for knowledge and in the application to wealth creation. We have already identified the process of continuing wealth-creation as the mainspring of modern Western Civilisation, providing its extraordinary power and dynamism. But the force which wound up this mainspring, which gave it its peculiar intensity and endurance, was puritanism. Without the puritan qualities, modern civilisation could not have completed the intellectual revolution which made it possible to harness the enormous wealth-creating potential of the expanding European world. Adam Smith pointed out that 'Parsimony, and not industry, is the immediate cause of the increase of capital',[5] summing up in the word 'parsimony' those qualities of frugality, application, and willingness to invest profits in the creation of further wealth, which we have associated with puritanism. The great machine of wealth-creation constructed by Western Civilisation did, in many respects, operate like a piece of clockwork. Without the qualities of zealous application through disciplined effort, however, the machine could not have been driven. Together with the possibilities for expansion opened up by the voyages of discovery, this spirit of puritanism directed the forces of wealth-creation in the formation of modern Industrial Civilisation.

We have come a long way in this chapter, covering a range of developments over three centuries that seem at first so diverse as to confound any attempt to bring them together in a constructive way. Yet behind the multitudinous diversity touched upon here in only the most superficial manner there is indeed a pattern: the pattern of a civilisation in process of explosive development, abandoning old constraints and seeking and finding new guides to conduct and achievement. Thus there is a unity of posture about the great developments of the period, in that they all appear for the first time to be looking to the future for some realisation of aspirations instead of the fading glories of the past. Even the fifteenth-century Renaissance, which began as a recovery of ancient wisdom, moved on to anticipate the evolution of new aspirations and art forms. Above all, the emergence of a new intellectual ethos, with a world-view which elevated rationality and wealth-creation, prepared the way for further innovation and introduced Western Civilisation to a new secular religion – the belief in progress.

6. The Promethean Revolution

Historians have adopted the myth of Prometheus as a useful image of modern industrialisation. According to the myth, Prometheus brought fire to earth by stealing it from the gods. He was punished for his crime by the gods, but they did not take back the gift with which Prometheus had enriched human life. By analogy, the agents of the process of industrialisation have immeasurably increased human prosperity, but a terrifying toll has been imposed as a result in the form of massive self-destruction through modern warfare. The image simplifies starkly both the achievements and the dangers of our civilisation. To see ourselves as the heirs of a 'Promethean Revolution' is thus an appropriate introduction to an examination of some of the complexities of modern industrialisation.[1]

It is necessary to speak of 'modern industrialisation' because we have already observed that a measure of industrial organisation has been a distinguishing feature of every civilised society. Without some degree of specialisation of function and application of skills to industrial and commercial enterprises, there can be none of the social differentiation, urbanisation, and generation of the more sophisticated cultural activities which are the distinctive features of civilised life. Thus industry of some sort is a very ancient and important feature of organised human societies. It probably began with the working of such comparatively simple materials as flint into blades and axe-heads which could then be used as trading commodities, and developed through the crafts of metal working into the intricate skills which became the closely-guarded secrets of corporations of guildsmen in the ancient civilisations and in medieval Europe. In all these pre-modern instances of industrialisation, however, there had been a stabilisation of growth at an early stage of development, due to conditions of political insecurity, or the limitation of the market, or the discouragement of powerful monopoly interests, or a combination of all these factors. What is so distinctive about modern industrialisation, on the other hand, is its capacity for apparently unlimited growth. Once the process had started, it rapidly outgrew the corporate institutions of medieval Europe and created new and more flexible institutions which could be adapted continuously to the expectation of perpetual growth. This process was partly a response to demographic pressures, but was more the result of the intellectual revolution of the sixteenth and seventeenth centuries, and particularly the new thinking about science and technology. It had momentous consequences in the transformation of life and of society.

The Demographic Factor

There is a hen and egg quality about the argument relating modern industrialisation to the large demographic changes which have occurred simultaneously in Europe since the beginning of the eighteenth century at least. The precise nature of the causal linkages remains obscure, but sufficient is apparent to demonstrate that the relationship is significant, and whether or not an increase in population causes industrialisation or is a consequence of it, it is certainly a factor deserving examination in an attempt to account for the distinctively dynamic nature of modern industrialisation.

As a starting point, it may be observed that there was widespread agreement in eighteenth century Europe that the population was increasing notably, and even alarmingly. Mercantilist governments had grown accustomed to welcoming an increase in population as a sign of national vitality and self-reliance, but following Adam Smith's systematic analysis of the economic weaknesses of mercantilist thinking a more critical view of population pressures began to prevail. This view was stated in its classic form by the Rev. T. R. Malthus in his *Essay on the Principle of Population* of 1798. Even before exact statistical data became available with the first British national census in 1801, Malthus was able to make realistic estimates of population growth and to calculate the likely rates of increase in the future. The gloomy conclusion to this exercise was that the population of the world was increasing faster than the resources available to feed the new mouths. Malthus therefore predicted that, unless the 'natural' checks of disease and war were able to contain the speed of population growth, 'gigantic inevitable famine' would ensue.

This prognostication sparked off a controversy about the capacity of the world to support an expanding population which has continued to the present, and there can be little doubt that it remains a problem of vital concern today. Several points are worth making about the controversy. In the first place, Malthus was stating a logical, mathematical, fact: *if* two lines of development converged, *then* certain results would follow. Although he tended to take a sombre view, he was not entirely deterministic about such a convergence. He was prepared to admit that a measure of self-discipline could arrest the rate of population growth and thus delay or even prevent the crisis. But his statistical equation remains applicable to all human societies, and only the introduction of new natural or human factors will change its logic. Secondly, one of the new factors which was not anticipated by Malthus was the capacity of industrialisation to increase productivity, so that the availability of resources was able to keep in pace with population increase, and eventually to outstrip it so that the inhabitants of industrial societies, although growing in number, could be supported at an increasing standard of living. This has been the greatest of all the achievements of industrialisation, and it has allowed world leaders to push the Malthusian nightmare to the back of their minds for a generation. Even though it had been demonstrated, in Ireland during the mid-nineteenth-century potato famine and elsewhere, that over-population remained a danger, such examples only served to confirm the view that societies which benefited fully from industrialisation had found a solution to the problem. Thirdly, however, the nightmare has reasserted itself in our own time, because the effect of industrialisation on many of the less developed parts of the world has been greatly to reduce the death rate by modern drugs and medical attention, without a commensurate increase in productivity. The result has been that the spectre of gigantic inevitable famine has emerged once more as a threat to the world community.

The work of Malthus served to focus the attention of statesmen, religious leaders, and academics, on the problems of demographic change. Once the fact of rapid population increase had been recognised, it prompted research into the mechanics of the process and speculation about the way in which it could be controlled. Regarding the mechanics, it is logically clear that an increase in population can be caused by a rise in the birth rate or a fall in the death rate or an excess of immigration over emigration – or by a combination of these three factors. At the point when the British growth in numbers became noticeable, in the eighteenth century – and in this as in other respects Britain led the world in the experience of continuing industrialisation – it is difficult to determine the relationship between these influences. But the general consensus of opinion amongst historians of population seems now to take the view that even though there appears to have been a slight rise in the birth rate in the middle of the century, the main impetus to the growth of population came from a steady fall in the death rate. This in turn has been attributed in the first instance to a dietary factor: people were eating better than their predecessors, in both quantity and quality of food, as a result both of improvements in domestic food production and of the importation of foreign goods which stemmed from the flourishing commerce of the mercantilist trading system. Judged by modern standards the food available to the average family in the eighteenth century was extremely poor, but what was statistically significant was the banishment of endemic famine and the provision of adequate food to keep more people, and particularly the very young, alive who would previously have died.

Once the increase in population had been recognised, again, it stimulated a range of important economic activities. The rising numbers may have presented more mouths to feed, but they also provided more hands to produce wealth and an enlarged market for the sale of manufactured commodities. The circular tendency of this argument will be apparent, but despite the difficulty of distinguishing cause and effect in this developmental sequence, the case for the existence of an intimate – and positive – relationship between population growth and industrialisation is overwhelming. The case is not weakened by the recognition that it was not an inevitable relationship, for when population growth occurred without the corresponding industrialisation, as in Ireland, the result was catastrophic. However, the positive relationship which may be taken as established for the successful industrial societies is not a constant one. It seems that every industrialising society, by inducing a rise in the standard of living which is welcome to members of that society, produces thereby a retardation in the birth rate as families seek to secure their living standards by restricting their numbers. A drastic reduction in the birth rate more than offsets a continuing decline in the death rate, as standards of medical care and hygiene improve, to cause a stabilisation in the level of population. In this way advanced industrial societies have brought about the 'demographic transition' which has enabled them to retain high levels of prosperity in large but stabilised populations.

This success of advanced industrial societies through deliberate family limitation seemed in the early twentieth century to be the final refutation of the dire prophecies of Parson Malthus. But subsequent events have demonstrated that the modern world cannot afford to forget the Malthusian nightmare, because the spread of sophisticated western medical facilities and of policies for the elimination of endemic diseases such as malaria and smallpox have produced a colossal population explosion in those parts of the world which have not yet acquired the benefits of increased productivity from industrialisation. In conditions of a declining standard of living, the virtues of family limitation are not apparent, for increased numbers are seen as some measure of insurance against an uncertain future rather than as extra mouths to be fed. In south-east Asia, Latin America, and large parts of Africa, the future of the whole policy of industrialisation has come to hinge on the possibility of inducing a demographic transition in societies which, in terms of standards of living, are not yet ready to accept it. Unless this can be achieved it seems likely that the Malthusian checks of disease, war, and gigantic inevitable famine will be back with us on a global scale.[2]

The Technological Impetus

Technology, the skills of making and doing things of service to society, is older than science, the systematic study of the human environment. In fact, if man is defined as *homo faber*, the tool-making animal, technology is as old as man, whereas science, which relies on a degree of literacy and numeracy in order to produce a cumulative record of data, is only as old as civilisation. Throughout its long history, technology has shown considerable independence of scientific endeavours, frequently relying instead on tradition, folklore, ritual, and even magic. This essentially repetitive, irrational, tradition of technology, has been gradually transformed by the application of scientific rationality, and particularly since the widespread acceptance of the Baconian view of science that its object is to promote the domination of man over his physical environment. Whereas techniques had developed steadily during the Middle Ages in response to specific social needs – improved water wheels and windmills, the improved sailing ships, the mechanical clock, printing with movable type, and so on – the successes of the new science of the seventeenth century created an intellectual environment favourable to technological innovation and provided essential information for the emergence of new techniques. Technology thus acquired a new impetus which made it an indispensable part of the process of continuing wealth-creation and industrialisation.

It was appropriate, in view of the Promethean quality of this process, that the first gift of the new technology to society should have been the fire engine: a prime mover capable of harnessing 'the Impellent Force of Fire'.[3] One of the pressing needs of the putative industries of the seventeenth century was cheap fuel, and in those parts of Europe such as England where the forests were already vanishing the obvious alternative to wood fuels was coal. But abundant coal depended on mining techniques which were in turn limited by the ability of their primitive pumps to remove the water that accumulated in deep workings. An engine capable of overcoming this handicap would unlock the supplies of cheap coal under the ground and make them available for a market which was increasingly hungry for fuel. This is what the fire engine – soon to become known by its more familiar name as the steam engine – did for industry at the beginning of the eighteenth century. It was thus an invention of tremendous significance, and one that could not have occurred without a series of scientific investigations which had explored the weight of the atmosphere, the power of a vacuum, and the elasticity of steam.

The precise links between these researches and the early inventors of the steam engine have been a matter of uncertainty and of controversy amongst scholars. The fact is beyond dispute that Thomas Newcomen, the prime inventor of the first efficient steam engine, was a blacksmith in Dartmouth who was personally far-removed from the scientists of the Royal Society. But it is significant that Newcomen was literate and that he was a nonconformist, at a time when the discoveries of scientists were becoming available to a literate public through the publications of the Royal Society and other media. English nonconformist sects formed networks of contacts in industry and commerce which were frequently nationwide, and which served as a ready means of communication for information about market requirements and scientific discoveries with practical possibilities. However much Newcomen and his associates may have seemed to fit the category of lowly mechanics in the social scale, therefore, there can be little doubt that they had access to the scientific information necessary for their purposes. To say this in no way detracts from their genius in being able to make successful application of the information at their disposal: it merely places them in their social context and shows how society and the attitude towards invention was being transformed by the powerful influences of the new science and a quest for the formula of continuous wealth-creation.

Another point deserves to be made about the social environment within which the epoch-making invention of the steam engine occurred. It is that the distinction between science and technology which has become conventional in the twentieth century should only be applied with caution to periods before the middle of the nineteenth century. Of course, a distinction can be made – and has already been made in this chapter – which traces the roots of science and technology to the beginnings of civilisation and to the origin of human species respectively. But these distinctions were not in-stitutionalised in the sense in which we have grown used to distinguishing between scientists and engineers in contemporary society. True, the skills of metal working and such-like became the specialised concerns of communities of craftsmen in ancient civilis-ation, whereas the pursuit of early scientific exercises was the province of priest-clerks who had the necessary skills of literacy and numeracy. But by the seventeenth century, any such distinction had become hopelessly confused in Western Civilisation. This was partly due to the highly practical motivation of many monastic com-munities, which had made unfashionable the classical distaste for manual work and had given a higher status to the skilled craftsmen. It was also the result in part of the absence of any tradition of slavery in Western Civilisation (at least in the European heartland), which avoided the denigration of manual work. Much more important, however, was the attitude of the bustling new 'middling' classes of Western Europe who seized so much of the initiative in the developments after 1500 both in the political affairs of the nation states and in the expanding commercial, industrial, and cultural activities. These middling classes were the primary agents of change towards a society of continuing wealth-creation, and they adopted both science and technology in so far as they served this objective. In the seventeenth and eighteenth centuries there was a conjunction of the two lines of development. Gentlemen scientists respected skilful craftsmen who made their instruments and conducted investigations for them. The inventive mechanic could win recognition for his scientific discoveries, and the natural philosopher could apply his ingenuity to mechanical invention, with equal ease and success. The Promethean Revolution was a product of this conjunction, and one of its major achievements was the steam engine.

This happy coincidence between the scientific and technological endeavours was undermined by their success, because as they expanded the need for specialisation intensified and each specialised group acquired its own institutional form which tended to mark out clear lines of demarcation, not only between science and technology but also between different sciences and technologies. It is pointless to regret this tendency, because a highly industrialised society clearly requires a vast amount of administrative organisation for which the differentiation of specialist skills is necessary. But it is important to realise the relative novelty of this intensity of specialisation, and to recognise that the institutions which have given it form and the educational system which has developed around it are the products of little more than 100 years. Before then the relationship was much more flexible – even the word 'scientist' was not invented until the 1830s, and any art or craft could be regarded as a 'technology' – although the price of this flexibility was a lack of institutional continuity or academic recognition which was too great for a developing industrial society to accept for long. So whereas the Royal Society in its first 150 years had been a body of catholic interests and inclusive preoccupations, the wealth of new institutions in the nineteenth century covering the various engineering and scientific professions compelled it to become, like them, more exclusive and limited in its interests. At the same time, the new apparatus of scientific education which steadily won acceptance in the new – and old – universities was distinguished from the more lowly provision which was made for technical and technological education.

Industrialisation

The recognition of the role of technology in the generation of wealth provided the impetus for a complicated series of industrial and social changes. So far only one invention has been mentioned, albeit the first and most important whereby the power of fire was harnessed in the service of man, and only one use of that invention, for pumping water out of coal mines. The immense service of the steam engine spread to every facet of industrial activity, for it came to provide motive power for the wheels of virtually every industrial process, and in the form of the railway locomotive and steam ship brought about a transport revolution. But science and technology produced other prime movers such as the internal combustion engine which took over and expanded even this great achievement, and other machines and processes which transformed the productive capacity of industry. Adam Smith had drawn attention to the power of specialisation to increase productivity, by making best use of every workman's talents, but the efficacy of specialisation was multiplied many times by mechanisation. It has been through mechanisation that the technological impetus has made itself felt in the process of industrialisation, and this achievement must be reviewed.

Agriculture, it may be argued, is the basic industry of a pre-industrial society. Stated in this apparently contradictory manner, the proposition spotlights the distinction between modern industrial society and the industries of earlier societies, the point of this distinction being that modern industries are essentially dynamic and cumulative while previous industries are stable and repetitive. Traditional agriculture, with its cyclical seasonal rhythms, epitomised these qualities. Nevertheless, as a form of productive organisation, agriculture deserves to be considered as an industry, and with the emergence of the new orientation towards continuing wealth creation agricultural organisation showed itself to be as susceptible as any other industrial process to the transforming forces. The structural reorganisation of British farms was made possible by the enclosure legislation, and the compact farms which resulted from this change were admirably suited for experiments in crop rotation, in the introduction of new crops, and in animal breeding. Like any other industry, agriculture responded to the increasing market for food provided by a rising population. Like any other industry, also, it was the subject of investment and, eventually, of mechanisation. The comparatively small size of most British farms was for a time a disincentive to mechanisation, but when techniques of mechanical harvesting had been pioneered in America and elsewhere they were introduced in Britain, and in the ingenuity in which the steam engine could be adapted to ploughing and threshing, many British farms took the lead. Improvements in world transport systems in the second half of the nineteenth century brought remaining traditional practices in agriculture under pressure from international competition, and compelled farmers to move towards more intensely specialised types of activity. In the new world economy, grains could best be grown on the large farmlands of the prairies, while the farms close to the centres of population tended to concentrate on meat, dairy production, and fresh fruit and vegetables. In the twentieth century, the availability of electricity and the internal combustion engine has stimulated continued concentration on increasing productivity, so that the phrase 'factory farming' has been coined to describe a general attitude towards agriculture. Even though it can no longer claim to be the leading industry, therefore, agriculture has demonstrated vividly the capacity to adjust to the dynamic needs of modern industrial society, and it remains a basic industry in the sense that provision of food is a fundamental requirement of any society.

The industries which showed the most immediate response to the new technological impetus in the eighteenth century were those concerned with the exploitation of coal, metal, and other mineral resources, which required mining techniques. It was in these processes that the steam engine fulfilled its first urgent social need by pumping water from deep shafts in coal and tin mines, thus permitting their more intensive exploitation. Successful metal mining with steam power had to await the development of the more economical Watt-type steam engine in the last quarter of the century, but British coal production was able to commence a dizzy rise in output which did not slacken off from the introduction of the first Newcomen engines to the outbreak of World War I. In the course of this expansion, the steam engine was harnessed to provide winding and locomotive power for the coal industry. Demand for coal slackened with the spread of internal combustion engines and the adoption of oil fuels, but was replaced by an even more meteoric industrial development, as the oil fields of the world were explored and exploited. Meanwhile, the search for other mineral deposits has proceeded all over the land surface of the earth, as well as under the sea on the continental shelf off Europe and America, and even the floor of the deep ocean has been examined for its possible riches. So many of the materials won from the earth's crust in this way are irreplaceable – particularly the fossil fuels – that concern is growing about their eventual depletion at some time in the quite near future. Such anxiety has not yet had a marked effect in controlling either the search for or the exploitation of these treasures, so that the extractive industries remain colossal enterprises dominant in the economy of industrialised societies.

The other great range of industries to experience the quickening influence of rising population, growing markets, and technological innovation, were the manufacturing industries. Many of these derived from old-established craft industries, operated on a small scale with little change over several centuries to provide the manufactured commodities for town markets. Some, however, were new to the period of mercantile expansion, depending on imported raw materials such as sugar, tobacco, and cotton, which had not been available in Europe before. These generally were less constricted by traditional patterns of operation than the older crafts, and were thus more amenable to rapid development by the application of investments, business enterprise, and new inventions. The cotton industry especially flourished in Britain in these conditions, and commenced in the second half of the eighteenth century a spectacular development which transformed the landscape of South Lancashire and other parts of the country and provided a model of a novel type of dynamic industry. The lesson did not need to be laboured in the economic and intellectual climate of Britain after 1750, so that the model was applied with vigour to a wide range of other manufacturing processes including textiles such as wool and silk, iron and steel, engineering, pottery, glass-making, and the manufacture of food and drink. Even the process of milling corn, possibly the oldest of food industries, was transformed first by the application of steam power to the grindstones and then by the substitution of rollers for grindstones in large dockside establishments so that flour could be manufactured in bulk from imported grain. At every level of manufacturing industry the pattern was reproduced: large factories, mechanical power, and new machines, which together vastly increased the productivity of the people engaged in the process and provided a supply of basic commodities – bread, beer, fabrics, clothes, shoes, pots and pans, pins and nails – for both the domestic and export markets. The new prosperity of industrialised societies became most apparent through this stream of manufactured commodities as they became widely available at low prices.

All these industrial processes were sustained and encouraged by associated developments in financial and commercial services such as banking, and by the rapid improvements in transport and communications which accompanied them. Transport facilities, in particular, responded to the needs of the new industries by providing a network of usable roads, canals, and railways. They did it by the same sort of application of resources – investment, enterprise, and technological innovation – which were so successfully transforming the other industries. The steam engine was applied to railways in what was to become its most picturesque and memorable form – the giant steam locomotives which dominated the railroads of the world until the middle of the twentieth century. Steam power also revolutionised sea transport, once the basic operating difficulties of building a sufficiently compact engine with economy of fuel had been overcome. This point was not reached with confidence until the second half of the nineteenth century, when the introduction of compound engines in screw-driven iron ships made it possible for steam ships to win over even the long-distance freight traffic onto which the sailing clippers had hitherto managed to hold. A corresponding revolution in communications, with the electric telegraph, the telephone, the radio, and television following each other in relentless succession, and the application of electricity and internal combustion to further improvements in transport, leading to the legion of mechanically powered road vehicles and the generation of the aeroplane, have maintained the momentum of change. The net result of these developments has been a transformation in the facility for movement and communication which would have been frankly inconceivable 200 years ago, and the consequences for both industrial and social organisation have been momentous.

The Transformation of Society

It is clear that a change in the scale and intensity of industry such as we have been considering could not have taken place without equally dramatic changes in the nexus of social relationships which encompassed it. For like every other social phenomenon, industrialisation is about people, and with the titanic changes in organisation which the new industrial processes and transport systems required it was inevitable that people would have to change their habits of life and that these changes would be accompanied by social dislocation and suffering. The whole of society, in short, was transformed by industrialisation.

The most immediate visual evidence of this transformation was urbanisation. An industrial society copes with the increase in its population by concentrating it in towns and cities. Such a response is only possible because the needs of industry generate a high degree of specialisation which allows people to withdraw from the primary activity of agriculture. Without specialisation, any growth of population presses upon existing resources and the Malthusian conditions are fulfilled, but once it begins there is a strong tendency for specialist skills appropriate to particular industries to concentrate in factories, in housing settlements, and in towns, so that industrialisation gives a powerful stimulus to the growth of towns. Moreover, the concomitant industrialisation of agriculture makes farming more economical, and the consequent reduction in demand for rural labour has frequently contributed to the flow of population into the towns. A town, however, is more than a concentration of people. The transition from a large village to a small town occurs when most of the population is engaged in specifically non-rural activities, with its own market and other trading facilities, and usually with distinct administrative functions. From the earliest civilisations and the Greek *polis*, towns have provided the centre of government, trade, and cultural life for an extensive hinterland, and these activities have remained characteristic features of town life ever since. But the main growth-point of a town has been its industrial potential, and in particular, its ability to provide the conditions for the development of manufacturing industries. This has been the fertile ground in which the rapid urbanisation of the last 200 years has taken place.

Ancient cities were limited in their size by technological factors such as problems of water supply, waste disposal, and internal transport. Only in exceptional cases such as the metropolis of Imperial Rome were the resources available to build the aqueducts, pave the roads and provide the services to sustain a major city, and most towns remained small and compact until the nineteenth century. Not until then did the transport amenities begin to make possible significant extensions in the area covered by towns, and after the urban crisis of the first half of the century, when it seemed as if the rapidly growing new industrial towns would collapse owing to their inability to maintain law and order or to control disease, the provision of urban police forces and supplies of piped pure water enabled them to make giant strides into the neighbouring countryside. The modern urban explosion had begun, and it is significant that the British census of 1851 revealed that for the first time in history a nation had a majority of its population living in towns and cities. Successive improvements in transport and communications, and the continuing demand for the products of manufacturing industry, have sustained and accelerated the processes of urbanisation. The great modern megapolises of London and Los Angeles, Tokyo and New York, are no longer exceptional: they are the typical forms of industrial society, and they could not survive without the network of services and the plethora of industrial enterprises which sustain them. Writers of science fiction have had little difficulty in envisaging the sort of catastrophes which are likely to occur if any of these services break down or functions disappear. Urbanisation has become the essential and indispensable way of life for most people in modern industrial society, yet it is a fragile structure depending on the interrelationship of many parts, damage to any one of which being able to disrupt the smooth operation of the whole.

The shift of population from the countryside to the towns, and the emergence of urbanisation as the typical life pattern of industrial society, has been accompanied by other profound social changes. For one thing, the customary allegiances, duties, and expectations of a rural community have disappeared. The traditional respect for the landowner and the priest, and the self-sustaining charitable relationships which are possible within a stable society, were both destroyed by the transition to town life. In their place, the rural migrant into the towns found freedom from many of the old constraints, but he also found anonymity and lack of concern. He was left largely to his own devices, but was free to starve without anybody caring to help him. If he could find work – and it was often the opportunity for employment which drew him to the town in the first place – the chances were that it would be the unfamiliar regimented employment of the factory or large establishment. If he could find a home, the chance of it being anything other than an overcrowded tenement in a squalid district was very slim. The new towns were usually able to offer a livelihood to the families which crowded into them, but they did so at a price, and this price included long hours of disciplined repetitive work, poor housing, and the loss of all those social contacts which had made rural life bearable even when it was impoverished.

While urbanisation destroyed traditional ways of life, however, it created new ones. The teeming ghettos of people trapped in industrial employment by a subsistence wage which enabled them to survive physically but curtailed their opportunities for choice, fashioned new loyalties. The traditional vertical integration of society, which was possible when people knew personally their social 'superiors' and their social dependents, and were bound to both by links of service, patronage, and personal loyalty, were replaced by a society which was integrated horizontally into clearly defined strata or, to use the term which became current in this usage around the middle of the nineteenth century, into social classes. The origin of the concept of social class has been the subject of recent scholarly debate, and there still are some complex issues which have not been satisfactorily resolved in this discussion. However, there seems to be general agreement about the novelty of the term in nineteenth-century Britain, and about its relationship with the rapid in-dustrialisation and urbanisation of the period. There is also a reasonable amount of agreement that working-class self-consciousness became apparent after the French wars ended in 1815, and that a similar identity of middle-class sentiment emerged about the same time.[4] What is not clear is the measure of class cohesion which is necessary to generate class consciousness. It soon becomes apparent on investigation, for example, that despite the disap-pearance of the vertical links of the old craft industries between master, workman, and apprentice, strong residual craft loyalties remained. Skilled workers, in particular, felt themselves to be differentiated from 'the great unwashed' of the unskilled masses, and they enjoyed considerable success in the later nineteenth century in organising their own protection and welfare through powerful trade unions and friendly societies. Also, strong regional loyalties persisted and made it difficult to combine the interests of groups such as Durham coal miners and Cornish china clay workers who in terms of employment could be regarded as closely linked. When it came to establishing class links across national barriers, it proved to be virtually impossible as the call to patriotism regularly prevailed over the loyalty of class consciousness. This fact was brought home starkly to leaders of working-class organisations at the outbreak of international hostilities in 1914.

The concept of social class has become even more problematic in the mid-twentieth century with the differentiation of the middle classes, who did so much to promote the rapid industrialisation two centuries before, into a wide range of different functions. In place of the business entrepreneur, building up his enterprise by a mixture of dedication, skill, and ruthlessness, the typical middle-class figure became a mixture of administrator, professional man, and salaried agent acting on behalf of a committee or a corporation. Twentieth-century commentators on this process have introduced the idea of a 'managerial revolution' whereby a range of management functions has been introduced between the traditional middle and working classes, blurring the distinctions and cushioning the conflict between them.[5] There can be little doubt that some such development has taken place, linked with the growth of giant corporations and with the separation of ownership from control so that the shareholders in a large enterprise, although they remain the legal owners of it, in fact are obliged by the size and complexity of the business to leave the management in the hands of salaried officers. The result of this process has been that people in an extraordinarily wide range of occupations have come to regard themselves as 'middle class'.

These are only a few of the difficulties associated with the concept of social class. It might be objected that class is not so much a matter of what people feel about their social relationships as an objective statement about how they stand in relation to the factors of production, and that when the chips are down every person can be classified as either a capitalist or a worker by hand or brain, as an expropriator or as one who is being expropriated. The objection must be considered because it stems from the Marxist critique of modern industrial society which continues to enjoy a remarkable vogue amongst commentators on society almost a hundred years after the death of its creator. Karl Marx certainly deserves to be taken seriously. He was the greatest prophetic figure of the nineteenth century, applying outstanding talents of perception and analysis to the social transformation of his time, and inveighing against the suffering that it caused. He characterised the economic system of Britain in the mid-nineteenth century as 'the capitalist mode of production' and he devised a technique of dialectical argument in order to show that this system was the result of a process of historical evolution and to demonstrate, moreover, that the system contained the seeds of its own inevitable decay and replacement by another (and superior) system. The dialectic was a technique borrowed from the German philosopher Hegel, who had deeply influenced Marx in his younger days, but it was applied in a context of historical materialism which was quite different from Hegel's attempt to show the more abstract evolution of ideas. Marx's dialectical materialism purported to show that all history, in the words of the *Communist Manifesto* of 1848, is 'the history of class conflict'.[6] According to this analysis, changing modes of production generate new classes which, like the thesis and antithesis of the Hegelian model, come into conflict and produce a new synthesis. But unlike Hegel, Marx saw the conflict as a concrete historical event – a social revolution – and the synthesis as a new mode of production superior to those that had preceded it. On Marx's historical scenario there had been a series of such social revolutions of which the bourgeois revolution was the latest, and the proletarian revolution was daily anticipated. The bourgeois revolution had occurred in Britain in the seventeenth century and had introduced the capitalist mode of production. On this analysis, it was clear that the proletarian revolution could be expected to take place in the same country, as this was the leading industrial nation in the world and should have produced the conditions which were most conducive to the next transition.

Critics of Marx have enjoyed themselves observing that the proletarian revolution did not occur where Marx predicted that it would, and that when it did occur – although then only in a form modified by Lenin to suit the particular circumstances of his situation – it did so in the most backward country in Europe, and one which was predominantly rural. It has also been observed that Marx's attempts to categorise early stages of civilisation in terms of class conflict involve such gross simplifications that they are untenable. Nevertheless, the extreme skill and subtlety of Marx's analysis of modern industrial society, and his demonstration of the relationship between economic forces and social forms, remain a model to succeeding investigators. A legion of disciples and would-be interpreters has arisen to justify his predictions and to contrive adjustments to the analysis by which the forecasts can be shown more satisfactorily to have been fulfilled. Certainly Marx does not lack for followers at the present day, although it is doubtful whether he would have welcomed them any more than those self-styled 'Marxists' of his own time from whom he tried to disassociate himself. From our point of view, the scholarly achievement of the man was beyond question, and it can be recognised that he gave a new depth to all forms of social investigation, which have remained in his debt. But in so far as Marx's doctrines retain something of the potency of a religious conviction today, it is necessary to make some judgement of his contribution to the theme of this book – the prospects of our civilisation.

Perhaps the first comment should be on the religious fervour of Marx's teaching. He aimed, after all, at establishing his analysis on the objective foundations of scientific method. But his work is infused by a deep sense of righteous indignation against the oppressors, of social compassion for the oppressed, and of messianic conviction that the forthcoming proletarian revolution will be not just a transition to yet another, better synthesis, but to an ushering in of the final stage of human evolution in which the need for the state and other instruments of oppression will wither away. All this shows a passionate involvement with his subject matter which transfers the analysis from the level of scientific examination to one of prophecy, and as a religious-style statement about orientation and objectives it needs to be treated with caution because of its susceptibility to subjective, personal factors. From our point of view, while the personal bias of Marx should be regarded with much sympathy, it is not possible to accept his black and white distinction between the good and the bad classes, or to identify with his vision of a Promised Land beyond the proletarian revolution.

Other comments follow from this. Marx's habit of associating the good with the proletariat and the bad with the capitalist bourgeoisie reveals a moral distinction that is too simple, and calls in question the moral assumptions which underlie the whole analysis. In particular, it is unscientific – in the sense that there is no evidence to support the belief – to maintain that human beings will behave better after the proletarian revolution. Such evidence as has become available since the Bolshevik Revolution of 1917 suggests just the contrary. Marx's idea of the state as an organ of oppression may be dismissed as a curious remnant of Victorian liberalism, but the Victorian liberals were not so naïve as to think that the state would eventually wither away: they strove for a minimal state, but not for a non-state. There is no doubt that the state can be used oppressively, but the alternative to the state is anarchy and no society can long survive anarchy. The object of all government is to regulate conduct between members of the state, so that good tendencies can be encouraged and bad tendencies can be controlled. It is unreasonable to expect any change in human nature that will make such controls unnecessary. Thus Marx's doctrine of human moral propensities must be judged and dismissed as simplistic.

Just as Marx was too ready to envisage moral reformation, so he was too willing to apportion blame. His terminology was partly responsible for this, though not so much in the use of 'proletariat' and 'bourgeoisie' instead of 'working class' and 'middle class', even though this choice gives a spurious conceptual quality to what should be practical designations. The real bogey is Marx's use of 'capital'. Admittedly, he was not alone in his delineation of a 'capitalist system', but Marx did it so much more thoroughly and persuasively than anybody else that his use of the term has become widely accepted, to the general confusion of debate. To Marx, capital was the outstanding instrument of class oppression, and by applying the label to the organisation of modern industrial society he made the overthrow of this organisation, as the capitalist system, the primary object of the proletarian revolution. But this use necessitated a distinction between modern society and the preceding phase of 'petty commodity production' which is not valid. There was, of course, a distinction, as we have seen, but it was one of scale rather than of quality, and the early phases of industrialisation were as much dependent on capital – in its simple common-sense meaning of wealth saved from consumption and invested in production – as those of the last 200 years. Capital may be in good hands or bad hands, but it is essential for any form of industrial organisation and Marx did a great disservice to posterity by making it difficult to see capital as a neutral term rather than one carrying overtones of moral condemnation.

Finally, and developing the same point, it should be pointed out that Marx offered no viable alternative to the capitalism which he condemned. He observed the transition from a comparatively stable social organisation to one which is highly dynamic, but it is never made clear to what the next transition – that of the proletarian revolution – leads. It is hardly a reversion to a stable agrarian type of society, although there are overtones of men living at peace, each with his own half acre and cow. Yet by condemning the process which is logically at the heart of industrial organisation he makes it virtually impossible to be anything other than a reversion to a more primitive form of life. The nonsense of this position has been demonstrated by the complete failure of all those societies which claim to have experienced the proletarian revolution to escape either from the need for a state or the need for capitalist procedures of saving and investment, even though they are generally performed by the state. This demonstration was not available to Marx, but that does not exonerate him from the charge of intellectual bankruptcy as far as his future projections were concerned. However brilliant his observation of the internal mechanics of modern industrial society, therefore, Marx has little to offer us in projecting the real possibilities which await our civilisation in the last quarter of the twentieth century and beyond.

In concluding this discussion of the social transformation wrought by modern industrialisation, it is worth stressing the dramatic improvement that has been made possible in the standards of life of citizens of industrial societies. To say this is not to ignore the fact that millions of people in the less developed parts of the world community do not as yet share in this improvement, or even that the distribution of comparative affluence in the developed countries is frequently very inequitable. It is merely to draw attention to the salient achievement of our civilisation: its outstanding success in providing the possibility of a rising standard of living for an ever increasing population. This has been done by a continuing growth in productivity through industrial organisation, as outlined in this chapter. The conversion of the industrial organisation to a dynamic process of self-sustaining growth has been a revolution of Promethean proportions. It has raised many problems of social adjustment, such as those concerned with class consciousness, which have still to be resolved. For all that, it has also created a model of aspiration and achievement for all the less developed countries, who are now asserting themselves to emulate the western nations in pursuit of the ethic of progress, which in this practical context means a higher material standard of living.

7. The Ascendancy of Europe

Physical expansion combined with rapid industrialisation to secure a period of world ascendancy for the nations of Europe. The period did not last long, as it was not achieved until the end of the eighteenth century and within 100 years other nations were learning the lessons of European success, which caused a relative decline in the influence of the states of Europe. Nevertheless, the dominance of Europe was not seriously challenged in the nineteenth century, and it is worth examining the qualities of this apotheosis in order to understand how the dynamic character of Western Civilisation was transferred to the scale of a world-wide phenomenon.

The Enlightenment

The nation states of modern Europe had been heavily embroiled, virtually from their outset in the sixteenth century, in religious wars which spread across the continent. We have already observed that many of the early nation states owed their development to the commitment which they made in this conflict, but when exhaustion brought the wars of religion to an end in the middle of the seventeenth century, the participant states found that they had acquired a secular autonomy not only in relation to their religious enemies but also in relation to the religion which they nominally supported. The claim of the Church, either Catholic or Protestant, to exercise some measure of control over the secular policy of the state, which had been taken for granted in the Middle Ages and survived throughout the active hostility of the religious wars, was henceforward seriously curtailed and in many cases reduced to vanishing point. The situation in England was typical: the established state Church became an 'erastian' institution, which is to say that it was regarded as an arm of government, taking its instructions from the secular authorities. The recognition of minority religions by the Toleration Act of 1689 brought a further diminution in the role of the established Church, and by the nineteenth century the functions of religious bodies had become predominantly ritualistic, although the Church of England retained some potentiality for secular power both through the inclusion of bishops in the House of Lords and through the considerable influence exerted in local government, at least in country parishes, by the clergy. For all practical purposes, however, the churches had ceased to exercise power over the secular state.

There are indications that this process of secularisation would have occurred even without the upheaval of the Reformation, as the advice given by Machiavelli to the princes of Florence about how to run their political affairs became a byword for cynical devotion to the achievement of power without religious or moral scruples. What the wars of religion did, however, was to generalise a set of maxims which had been applicable in the first instance only to the Italian city-states, and to enhance the nation-states as much larger vehicles of the same doctrine of autonomous, secular, sovereignty. Successive political philosophers: Bodin – Hobbes – Locke – Montesquieu: drew out the implications of such sovereignty, postulating the existence of autonomous states and showing how they could be expected to function. John Locke, in particular, made a decisive contribution to the new understanding of the state. Writing as a contemporary of Isaac Newton, he was deeply impressed by the mechanistic rules which appeared to govern the physical universe, and he used them both to destroy the remnants of the notion of the divine right of kings and to construct a mechanistic theory of the state. According to the latter, good government is determined by the existence of constitutional 'checks and balances' which, like the parts of a well-adjusted piece of clockwork, combine to keep the body politic in a healthy condition. This view led to the separation of powers in government between the executive, the legislature, and the judiciary. It had a powerful influence on constitutional thinking in the eighteenth century, most significantly in the forming of the American constitution.[1]

Locke was also responsible for popularising another idea that was to make an important contribution to the modern state. This was the idea of a social contract, according to which the original members of a society set down the terms of their mutual agreement to serve the collective purpose of the society. It was recognised that for many state societies the formulation of any such contract was a fiction, or at least that any record of it had been lost in the mists of antiquity. But it was maintained that a social contract was *implicit* in the existence of modern states, and in the absence of any acceptable alternative, the arguments of divine origin having been rejected, this was a very convincing thesis. So as well as establishing the mechanistic nature of the modern state, John Locke also provided a secular justification for the participation and representation of the citizens in the process of government. With the admission of this idea, the era of European liberalism could be said to have begun, because for the first time the individual citizen rather than the whole, the state, the party, or the family, became the object of political attention.

This is the background to the European 'Enlightenment', the intellectual mood which gradually replaced religious antagonism, deriving from a strong sense of the secular state and of natural science as a means of increasing knowledge, and rejecting religion together with other traditional authorities while turning with hope to the future for the continued unfolding of human progress. The thinking of the Enlightenment stressed rationality, system, and order. Its most characteristic manifestations were the militant rationalism of Voltaire and the compilations of the encyclopaedists who aimed at amassing human knowledge in a well-ordered and usable form. Considering the emphasis that it placed on individualism, it is remarkable that so little progress was made during the eighteenth-century hey-day of the Enlightenment towards more liberal forms of government. This, after all, was the period when the absolute power of monarchical government was taken for granted in most of the European nation states, with the France of Louis XIV setting the style of the *ancien régime*, and even such exponents of intellectual enlightenment as Voltaire depending to some extent upon the patronage of Frederick the Great of Prussia. Admittedly, Frederick and other monarchs of the period won themselves the style of being 'enlightened despots', but whatever the degree of their enlightenment – and it fluctuated widely – they remained firmly despots in matters of government and political representation. Even in England, although the power of absolute monarchy was permanently constricted after the seventeenth-century civil wars, the king remained the most important political figure and the limitations placed on him were wielded by a small clique of aristocrats and gentry who exercised power in London and in parliament.

Nevertheless, the spirit of enlightenment influenced even this seemingly unpromising ground. The idea of the rule of law was increasingly taken as the basis for political activity, and in England this had long roots going back to Magna Carta or, more probably, to a vision of Magna Carta which provided a convenient model for liberal aspirations from the early seventeenth century. Elsewhere, in Europe and America, demand for the recognition of the rule of law became a potent stimulus to novel thoughts about the state. Similarly, the enlightenment encouraged another staple ingredient of European liberalism: the search for social justice. This was the period in which serious thought about the individual began to raise doubts about the role of slavery in the colonial economy, and the lot of other oppressed or ill-treated groups such as the prison population. The application of rationality and scientific investigation to political conduct thus prepared the ground for some of the greatest political upheavals of Western Civilisation.

The Age of Revolutions

In a sense, the greatest achievement of the European Enlightenment was the American Revolution. Not only was the Revolution planned and carried through by a notable group of enlightened gentlemen such as Washington, Franklin, Jefferson, and Hamilton, but also the Constitution which emerged from the Revolution was an epitome of the political principles of the Enlightenment. The War of American Independence, moreover, was fought in a civilised way (as wars go) between rebellious colonists and a government which found many powerful voices speaking for the rebels at home, and it left remarkably little rancour to sour future relations between Great Britain and the United States. There was thus some cause to hope that the ways of rationality were triumphing over those of emotion, and that mankind had discovered a new and more orderly way of transacting political business.

The fact that this hope was not fulfilled is one of the most singular facts of modern European history, and it is not easy to summarise the reasons for the abrupt change in mood of the European intellect at the end of the eighteenth century. In the first place, however, it quickly became apparent that the American model of comparatively easy transition to constitutional and representative government was not directly applicable to any European situation. In America, the governmental forces were, for the most part, an ocean-width away, and the revolutionaries could carry through their plans without needing to dispose of a resident monarchy or aristocracy because they *were* the resident aristocracy. In Europe, on the other hand, the ruling classes were exceedingly well entrenched, and were not willing to go far towards recognising the aspirations for an extension of the rule of law and social justice which had been generated by the Enlightenment. France, in particular, which had been the spiritual home of the Enlightenment, was politically structured to make an American-style revolution impossible, although this did not become apparent until the events of the French Revolution had begun to run their course in 1789.

A second and possibly even more significant difference between the American Revolution and the European convulsions which followed it was the infusion of a potent ingredient of romanticism. The European Romantic Movement is not to be pinned down by a brief definition, but there is evidence of some striking developments in late eighteenth-century thought which ran directly counter to some of the principles of the Enlightenment. Although J. J. Rousseau had taken up the Enlightenment notion of a social contract, for instance, he imbued it with the romantic conception of the 'noble savage' who was enchained by his political relationships. The object of political aspiration was subtly influenced by this idea, away from increasing social order towards maximising individual freedom, which paradoxically involved forcing people to be free in order to articulate the needs of an abstract 'general will'. Likewise, the romantic reverence for the natural world ran counter to the mechanistic view of nature sponsored by the rationality of the Enlightenment: for romantics like William Blake, Newton represented the rule of mechanical calculation and was scornfully rejected. There was thus a resurgence of interest in the irrational, in emotion, in feeling, and in a sense of the organic wholeness of man's part in the cosmos. Such sentiments proved to be a fertile ground for the virulent nationalism which spread across Europe in the wake of the French revolutionary armies. Nationalism was stirred in France partly by the attack of her anti-revolutionary neighbours, but more by the romanticised conception of the aims of the Revolution. Once awakened, the very success of French nationalism promoted the rapid rise of nationalism amongst the other European states, and with its advent the whole temper of politics in Europe changed. Henceforward, the appeal to patriotism – 'my country right or wrong' – became one of the strongest sentiments of political intercourse, and it is largely the influence of Romanticism. Rousseau and Blake, Goethe and Wordsworth, Burke and Beethoven, differed in many respects, but they had one thing in common – they were all the intellectual products of a European movement that had turned its back on mechanistic rationality in favour of organic feeling for the good in tradition and the world of nature.

The effect of introducing the American model of enlightened revolution to Europe was thus to open a veritable Pandora's box of novel and unexpected forces, many of them incredibly violent even though some were beneficial. It seemed at first sight as if the principles of the American Declaration of Independence were neatly adopted by the French revolutionaries under the slogan of 'Liberty, Equality, and Fraternity', but practical experience revealed a dangerous ambivalence about these abstract concepts. 'Liberty' was one of the self-evident truths of the American founding fathers, and it subsumed the right of the citizen to representation, to the possession of property, and to the pursuit of happiness. These were the liberal principles incorporated in the new constitution of the United States, and they became immediately the birthright of all white Americans, being extended to other races later. They represented a very practical Anglo-Saxon notion of liberty. But in the heat of the French Revolution, the idea was transmuted into a different category of interpretation. It was separated from the idea of individual freedom and associated with the nation-state as a whole, so that 'Liberty' became an adjunct of the new nationalism. As such it was possible to disregard individual rights which ran counter to the current view (that of the prevailing administration) of the general will of the nation. At this level of abstraction the term had lost its 'liberal' connotations but acquired an animation which made it a battle-cry for every national aspiration in Europe.

It is important, in defining 'Liberty', to ask 'liberty to do what?' as the answer to the question will determine whether an Enlightenment view of individual freedoms or a Romantic view of group aspirations is appropriate. Similarly, an enquiry into 'Equality' should seek to distinguish the particular forms of equality appropriate to the discussion. As an abstraction, the concept is virtually devoid of meaning, although it is far from devoid of emotive content. In mathematical terms, equality has a clear meaning, as it does in many areas of natural science. But in social terms, 'equality' may relate to wealth, income, status, possessions, education, opportunities, and standard of living – to name only a few of the more obvious areas in which inequalities are measured, often according to indices of very questionable accuracy. The social equality to which the Enlightenment attached importance was equality before the law, which is fundamental to the achievement of the rule of law and is eminently measurable. In the full flood of romantic ardour unleashed by the French Revolution, however, such legal equality seemed less important than the removal of class inequalities between fellow-citizens, so that the demand for equality tended to focus on the removal of personal property as its objective. It is an objective which has proved to be illusory, because even overtly 'classless' societies have found it necessary to recreate levels of incentive and reward in order to function smoothly. Equality, therefore, remains a problematic concept of Western Civilisation. It has stimulated several generations of socialist thought, for whatever differences there are between socialists, and there *are* many, their common concern is a conviction that equality is important. Too frequently, however, they are less interested in the realisable equalities such as equality before the law, than in the intangible forms of equality which defy precise expression and add more heat than light to political discourse.[2]

There is an implicit logical progression in the revolutionary battle-cry 'Liberty! Equality! Fraternity!' Without the recognition of some measure of individual freedom, discussion of equality between the individuals of a society is a pointless exercise, and it is exactly this trap into which much of the argument about the extent of equality in the autocractic societies of modern communism has fallen. If the terms are to cease being abstractions and can be pinned down to a specific rather than a general meaning, an equality such as equality before the law involves liberty in the form of recognition as a responsible individual participating in government either directly or through representation. Similarly this is the case with 'Fraternity', the most elusive of the revolutionary aspirations. The myth of Cain and Abel reminds us that brotherly sentiments are not always kind, and the lesson has been reinforced by the viciousness of civil wars, but 'fraternal relations' normally carry overtones of brotherly love, and it was clearly with this intention that Fraternity was included amongst the objectives of successful revolution. As such it is a noble aspiration, for the only permanent peace amongst the brotherhood of mankind can come from an abundance of fraternal affection. But to pronounce support for fraternity, to say 'All men are brothers' without translating the abstraction into real terms as one's neighbour, the despised racial group, or the political adversary, is to empty it of meaning. Fraternity cannot begin to operate until all persons are recognised as having equal status as free citizens. Only in this cumulative sense can the abstractions of the revolutionary banners be converted into the real terms of political society.

The pursuit of revolutionary terminology has led us away from the discussion of the political revolutions which, beginning with the American and French Revolutions, make it possible to speak of nineteenth-century Europe as 'the Age of Revolutions'. Not that Europe in this period was in a condition of permanent political upheaval. Such was certainly not the case, although there were sporadic outbreaks of localised but significant revolutions, particularly in 1830, 1848, and 1870. The designation remains appropriate, however, because for a century after the ending of the French revolutionary wars in 1815, Europe remained under the influence of the revolutionary tradition. This was most apparent in the continued ferment of nationalism, producing new nation states in Belgium, Italy, and Germany, but it was also evident in the continuation of the debate about liberty, equality, and fraternity; and in the growth of strong radical movements animated by these ideals. Despite long periods of political stability and even stagnation, the governments of Europe throughout this century felt themselves permanently at risk from these revolutionary forces. Some of them were shaken by actual revolution. Others, like Britain, adjusted themselves gradually so that they incorporated a steadily increasing amount of the revolutionary objectives. Others, again, like Tsarist Russia, successfully repressed all such movements, only to generate explosive pressures which made the eventual revolution uncontrollable. Europe in the nineteenth century had become revolution-prone.

The Maturation of Democracy

Ever since the Greek city-states experimented with different forms of government and Greek philosophers analysed the components of these governments, there has been a democratic tradition. Admittedly, the success of Greek democracy was limited and the philosophers tended to be dismissive about its virtues, but in Classical Athens and many of the lesser Greek cities a democratic form of government did flourish for a time, with the citizens usually exercising a direct control over policy-making or selecting representatives to act for them. Only adult male free men were granted the status of citizens, women and slaves being specifically omitted, but within these limits government by the people worked, and it was seen to work at least as fairly and efficiently as other forms of government.

Despite Greek experience, however, democracy did not have much chance to develop in the two millennia following the conquests of Alexander and the rise of the Roman Empire. This was partly because of the unsettled conditions created by war and the need for centralised military authority under the administration of a conquering régime, and partly because of the prolonged breakdown of any except the simplest forms of government which followed the collapse of the western Roman Empire. But more important was the fact that democracy is a comparatively sophisticated form of government. Compared, that is, with forms of monarchy and aristocracy, democracy requires a high level of participation in government by the citizens, and such participation can only be achieved amongst a body of citizens who are responsible, aware of their own status, and ready to recognise the status of their fellows. These are complex conditions which do not come naturally or easily, but are the result of careful cultivation in civilised societies. They began to appear in some of the thriving city states of the late Middle Ages, and particularly the North Italian states such as Florence and Venice, but incipient democracy here was overwhelmed by the growth of the nation states, the wars of religion, and intense international rivalry. Only in the seventeenth century, in England, Holland, and some of the new trans-Atlantic colonies, did conditions favourable to a high level of democratic participation in government, begin to emerge once more.

Meanwhile, another significant development had occurred. If participation by the citizens in the process of government is seen as the *content* of democracy, its *form* may be expressed as the rule of law. It is possible to have a rule of law without participation in government (although it is unlikely that the rule of law will long remain intact in such conditions), but it is quite impractical to

consider democratic participation except in the constitutional context of a rule of law. The rule of law means more than the existence of
laws. Laws, after all, are a set of rules determined by that particular
form of society we call the state, and every state has its laws. The
dissolution of the laws of a state involves the dissolution of the state
itself, because these define the manner in which it fulfils its functions.
But laws are normally made by the governors and applied to the
governed, in such a way that the law-makers – monarch, party,
tyrant, ruling class – are exempt from its restrictive provisions. When
the rule of law operates, on the other hand, nobody is above the law.
All citizens, governors and governed alike, are subject to the same
legal requirements. The rule of law, moreover, lays down the
conditions by which the government can be changed and the law
modified. Such rules are essential to the democratic participation of
members in a voluntary society such as a trade union or a tennis club.
They are no less essential to the functioning of democratic participation in the state.

The rule of law, like democracy itself, has a long and honourable
ancestry, going back to the ancient Greeks, but also like democracy,
it has had a very chequered history. Under the Roman Empire there
was a great deal of law and legalism: the Romans were famous law-
givers. But as long as it was a law imposed by the Emperor or his
servants it was not the rule of law. Roman law later became one of the
main models of Western European law-makers, and it was most
frequently used by autocratic governments in order to devise an
efficient legal system. The other legal tradition of Western Civilisation was that of common law, based upon cumulative custom and
practice and consequently more susceptible to participatory evolution than Roman law. In England especially, the appeal to the
authority of legal precedents enshrining collective decisions and
statutory acts of parliament was made in the seventeenth century in
order to counter the appeal to divine right urged on behalf of the
monarch by James I and Charles I. This became, in effect, a claim for
the rule of law – an argument that not even the monarch or his
ministers could be exempted from the provisions of the law. The
claim was an anathema to the early Stuart kings, and contributed
powerfully to the outbreak of the Civil Wars which broke the
absolute power of monarchy and established in a preliminary and
tentative sense the rule of law in British government.[3] It remained
preliminary and tentative for well over a century, because the

structure of English society was not immediately conducive to the development of participatory democracy and it could not be maintained that the law applied equally to all ranks of society. Nevertheless, the principle of the supremacy of the law over the law-givers had been acknowledged, and this gave the opportunity for continuing modifications in the law which enabled it to extend its scope and to generalise its influence. It also ensured that, in a period of widening possibilities for social advancement through industry and commerce, and of increasing educational experience, there was sufficient legal flexibility to recognise the claims for a greater measure of participation in government. Form and content, the rule of law and the active participation in government, were thus able to grow together, so that by the mid-nineteenth century in Britain and the United States, democracy had become a feasible and even a desirable objective. For the first time since the Classical age of Greece, significant states had begun to commit themselves to a democratic form of government.

This coming to maturity of democracy has been the outstanding political achievement of the modern world, and deserves to be recognised as such despite the denigration of critics who fail to understand its importance or the contempt of those who take it for granted. It is worth while, therefore, reflecting on some aspects of this achievement. In the first place, it should be observed that it is by no means a peculiarly British quality, even though in some respects English experience led the world. But by drawing on the same roots in the rule of law as those of Britain, the American colonists in 1776 established the first constitution explicitly devoted to its maintenance and incorporated the intense participatory activity of the colonists themselves. The United States, indeed, was the first fully articulated democracy of modern times, although it remained outside the main theatre of western activity until the second half of the nineteenth century, by which time the American Civil War had served to eliminate the glaring inconsistency of slavery from the democratic aspirations of the nation. Also influenced by British and American precedents, France pursued a more violent course towards democracy between 1789 and 1870, fluctuating between autocratic monarchy and revolutionary anarchy but eventually achieving a mature political stability in the Third Republic. Other European nations followed even more erratic courses, but the trauma of Hitler's war served even to swing West Germany firmly towards democracy, and most of the nations of Western Europe are now committed to democratic forms of government.

This leads on to the second observation, which is to note the ambiguity which has crept into the term 'democracy' on account of its acceptance as a term of approval. The fact that large numbers of communist states and developing nations now style themselves democracies has threatened the value of the term. Of course, there is no reason why a communist or developing state should not be a democracy. But by the terms of the definition which has been implicit in this discussion, it is clear that many of them are not democracies, as they possess neither a rule of law nor a high level of citizen participation in the process of government. Can they be regarded as democracies in any other sense? It is time, perhaps, to make our definition more explicit. The first meaning of democracy – government by the people – is too general, because it is necessary to specify who are the people and what the processes of government imply. Regarding 'the people', it is surely not unreasonable in the conditions of the modern world to assert that these comprise the total members of a given society, or, in the case of states, 'the citizens'. The latter category is less than the total, as it excludes minors and temporarily disenfranchised groups, but must consist of the vast majority of adult members. Regarding involvement in 'government', it is essential that the citizens of a democracy should participate in the processes of decision-making which determine how the state is governed. But the modern state presents problems of size which were not apparent in the Greek city-states which were the first to practise democracy. In these early examples, it was possible for *direct* participation through mass meetings of the citizens. Nowadays, the mode of participation is more complex, requiring either *representative* participation through citizens elected to speak for many of their fellows; or *secondary* participation through voluntary societies (churches, trade unions, sports clubs, professional associations, welfare clubs, political parties, consumers' organisations, and pressure groups of all sorts). There is also a surviving element of *direct* representation, through the vote or the letter to the press, in even the largest democracy, and it is essential that all these modes of participation should function actively in a modern democratic state. None of them, it must be stressed, can endure for long unless they are guaranteed by a rule of law which ensures that no citizen, however important, will have a legal advantage over any other. Thus we arrive at a definition of democracy as a form of government recognising the rule of law and requiring the participation, in a variety of ways, of all the citizens in the processes of decision-making. By this definition it must be ruled most emphatically that the East European communist countries and the new states of Asia and Africa under the control of military juntas do not qualify. This is not necessarily a criticism, as there may be thoroughly valid reasons for them adopting their present forms of government. But it makes nonsense of the term democracy to apply it to states where the level of participation is minimal and where the rule of law does not exist.

A third observation takes up a point which has already been made: democracy is a sophisticated form of government. This follows inevitably from the participatory emphasis of democracy, because it is impossible to take an active and responsible part in any form of government without a measure of self-confidence and ability at speaking, reading, and writing. And these are the qualities of an educated society – one in which the citizens acquire a wide general knowledge and a skill in the literate arts in addition to the craft or vocation by which they earn their livelihood. Without these qualities of basic literacy, democracy will simply not work, as has been sadly exemplified by the collapse of the new democracies established in Asia and Africa in succession to the colonial régimes which paid too little attention to inculcating the skills necessary to sustain democracy. Without high standards of indigenous public service, without viable trade unions, with poor primary education and non-existent secondary education, democracy could not work. All these things take time to develop, and given time democracy may yet grow in places where it seems to have failed most abysmally. Meanwhile, it is important that democracy should not be discredited by the failures. It remains the best possible objective for the political aspirations of a developing country.

There is an interesting converse to the situation in the developing countries. It may be wondered whether there is a *necessary* correlation between democracy and the qualities of political sophistication which have been described. In particular, do high levels of education lead inevitably to democracy? There is certainly a tendency for people with a good education – that is, one of secondary standard or higher – to achieve the ability and self-confidence necessary to participate in the processes of government, and it is tempting therefore to identify a correspondence between industrialisation, with its dependence on a vast number of skills requiring intensive training, and democracy. This correspondence has led some commentators to look hopefully for signs of 'convergence' between the political systems of the great industrial powers of the world. But it has to be admitted that the signs of this convergence, if they exist at all, are at present well hidden. The advanced industrial states of the communist world, with the Soviet Union outstanding amongst them, have as yet made little attempt to adopt democratic forms of government in the sense defined above. There may be understandable reasons for this: a desire to keep clear of the police, or to enjoy a rising standard of living as quietly as possible, and, at a more rationalised level, a belief that government is best left to the experts. But the fact remains that democracy does not derive necessarily and inevitably from a high level of educational skills. There is even some reason to fear that modern educational goals, with their intense specialisation, may be reducing the capacity of people to participate democratically, and this is an anxiety to which we will return later. For the moment, it is sufficient to complete this discussion of democracy by indicating its fragility compared with other forms of government. It will not begin to grow until the appropriate level of sophistication has been achieved by the citizens, nor will it survive without their continued participation. It will not develop without the conscious cultivation of citizens who want it, and in its incipient forms it is an easy prey to the strong-arm tactics of the police state. The lesson of western experience is that democracy is a form of government which is pre-eminently desirable and appropriate to advanced industrial states, but that it will only flourish as a result of dedicated commitment on the part of the citizens.

The Apotheosis and Decline of European Hegemony

Through industrialisation and expansion, through the growth of powerful nation states and of intensive rivalry between them, and through the Enlightenment and a series of political and social convulsions, Western European Civilisation achieved an unprecedented world ascendancy. The dynamic quality of the achievement ensured that it could not last for long, because non-European powers were quick to learn the lessons to which European domination subjected them, and the logistics of world resources made it impossible to maintain domination once these lessons had been learnt. But while it lasted, European hegemony prepared the ground for several subsidiary attainments which included a period of comparative stability in world politics, the prosecution of a ruthless phase of imperial exploitation, and the widespread export of European culture.

Comparative political stability was established in Europe by the great powers which pacified the continent in 1815, after a generation of violent upheaval deriving from the French Revolution. The idea and the reality of revolution were by no means dead, as we have seen, but the dominant requirement of all the nations was peace and reconstruction so that the Congress of Vienna was able to work out a set of agreements which endured, with minor modifications, for ninety-nine years. Within the new European equilibrium, Britain and France remained jealous and suspicious of each other's intentions, but peace was maintained between them and they even entered an armed alliance against Russia in the Crimean War and were drawn steadily together by their mutual apprehensions about the rapid growth of Imperial Germany once Bismarck had initiated a Prussian-led process of German unification. Simultaneously, anxiety increased amongst the western powers about the policy of Tsarist Russia in East Europe and India, and about the dangerous power vacuum which was appearing with the internal decay of the Turkish Empire. Apart from the brief escapade of the Crimean War and the sharp conflict of the Franco-Prussian War, however, Europe enjoyed a century of peace which contrasted strongly with the previous three centuries of almost continuous warfare.

While the 'Concert of Europe' preserved relative harmony on the continent, the British navy ensured a similar period of passivity in international affairs. Left by Nelson with complete dominance of the oceans of the world at the Battle of Trafalgar in 1805, Britain continued to exercise naval supremacy until 1914 and was able to assert the *Pax Britannica* whereby naval gunboats were readily available to protect British mercantile and colonial interests and to minimise the rivalry of other European powers. At first, such potential rivalry was diminished by the general war-weariness of the nation states, but also by a revulsion from the principles of the 'Old Colonial System' which sprang both from a close perusal of the doctrines of Adam Smith and from observing the course of events in the North American colonies of Britain. There was a widespread feeling that colonies ripened inevitably like fruit on a tree, and that when the time came for the fruit to fall it was pointless to try to prevent what was a natural process. The struggles of the Spanish American colonies to win their freedom received powerful support from such sentiments in Europe, and appeared as one more confirmation of the view that, as forms of investment for the parent country, colonies were simply not worth the candle.

This attitude was far from being one of defeatist resignation. It was rather a recognition that successful trading relationships did not rely on colonial dependence, and the tremendous boom in trade between Britain and North America after the colonies won their independence appeared amply to justify the new doctrines of Free Trade and *laissez-faire* – let every man conduct his own business according to his own best interests. Nevertheless, it could not be denied that colonies had certain uses, amongst which, in a generation made anxious by the spectre of the Malthusian population explosion, the prospect of finding empty territories for systematic settlement by communities of emigrating colonists, was the most pressing. Urged on by Gibbon Wakefield and other spokesmen of the utilitarian radicalism fashionable in the 1830s, Britain embarked on such a programme of systematic colonisation in Australia and New Zealand and, to a lesser extent, in South Africa.[4] In the latter case there was already a resident colonist population in the shape of the Dutch or Boer farmers, and conflict between the two communities caused the 'Great Trek' of the Boers into the interior of the High Veldt and the establishment of independent Boer republics in the Orange Free State and the Transvaal. In Australia and New Zealand, on the other hand, apart from small indigenous populations, the British settlers had the land to themselves and set about recreating the conditions of nineteenth-century British domesticity at the antipodes.

Thus, almost insensibly and with a minimum of government intervention, a new phase of imperial development began. The deliberate curtailment of participation by the government was apparent in the reception of Lord Durham's famous report on the Canadian colonies, which led to the first instalment of self-government in the 1830s and provided a model for the growth to independence for all colonies of white settlers. Elsewhere, the vast mercantile empire acquired by the British East India Company in India preserved the fiction of non-government intervention until the mutiny of 1857 which caused the government to take a new look at

British rule in the Indian sub-continent and led to a renewal of direct intervention. By this time, in any case, the mood was beginning to change again, as European rivalry in the late nineteenth century sought to guarantee the raw materials and markets for the industries of the leading nations, and especially those of Britain, France, and Germany. Nervousness and rivalry combined to bring about the rapid apportionment of the remaining unclaimed parts of the terrestrial land surface. France took the whole of the Sahara and moved into West and Central Africa. Germany acquired colonies in south-east and south-west Africa. Even Belgium snatched a colonial 'plum' in the Congo basin. But the lion's share was acquired by Britain, exploiting the advantage of its naval supremacy to promote colonies and to stimulate trade – even, if necessary, as in the case of China, by forcing reluctant eastern nations to enter into trading relationships. Thus was established the 'Mercator Empire' of Victorian Britain, whereby British possessions and dependencies, painted red on Mercator's projection of the world map with its progressive enlargement of territories towards the poles, gave a powerful impression of predominance.

The predominance was real, but short-lived. It was challenged, in the first place, by Britain's European rivals. British and French interests came into dangerous conflict in parts of Africa, and Germany, with its two foot-holds in southern Africa, paraded its sympathy with the Boer republics when these clashed with Britain. The Boer War was the last of a series of localised imperial wars conducted by Britain in Asia and Africa. It was exacerbated by the discovery of diamonds and gold within the frontiers of the Boer republics and the consequent flow of immigration, and also by the expansionist aspirations of the British government in South Africa under Cecil Rhodes, one of the most remarkable of the generation of late Victorian imperialists. The humiliation and eventual victory of Britain in the Boer War led to an attempt to temper imperial *hauteur* with compassion in a political union ensuring a high degree of independence for the Boers. In a sense, therefore, the Boer War marked the beginning of another form of challenge to British imperial predominance – a challenge from the indigenous population. In the course of the twentieth century, this challenge undermined the whole structure of Victorian imperialism and ensured its complete collapse.

Long before this collapse occurred, however, voices had been raised in protest against Victorian imperialism. It was pointed out by Liberal critics such as J. A. Hobson, and with even more vehemence by Marxist critics such as V. I. Lenin, that this late-nineteenth-century imperialism was based upon a fallacious understanding of the role of vast underdeveloped territories in the economy of the mother country. The promoters of imperialism such as Rhodes saw these areas as potential sources of raw materials and markets. Hobson was able to point out that they involved a colossal waste of resources in administering backward countries and compelling them to fit a pattern which their inhabitants – if any – did not wish to accept. He also observed that the contemporary infatuation with imperial adventures was diverting attention from much-needed domestic reforms, and was leading Europe into a dangerous area of conflict when it should have been moving towards greater internationalism. Lenin sharpened this analysis to present imperialism as an extreme form of capitalist exploitation designed both to take advantage of the weakness of the underdeveloped countries and to distract the proletariat at home from its revolutionary objectives. Imperialism, in short, came under mounting criticism in the twentieth century, and this contributed to the other influences causing its rapid decay. By the end of the war in 1945 all the great empires of the western powers were in collapse. Attempts to resurrect them by France and Holland failed painfully. Britain, on the other hand, accepted the process with relatively good grace and presided over the peaceful dismemberment of its own colonial empire.[5]

In retrospect, the period of high-imperialism from about 1870 to 1914, can be seen as the final stage of European ascendancy. Its slightly hysterical note, reflected in the literature of 'jingoism' and in the doctrine of 'the white man's burden', may be attributed partially to a feeling that it *was* the final stage, and that other powers were beginning to assert themselves in fields which had previously been the preserves of European influence and diplomacy. The growing power of the United States exemplified this sense of European loss of prestige, which the clamour about imperialism helped to obscure. The very success of European industrialisation ensured that, in the course of time, as the rest of the world adopted the lessons of European experience, the balance of world power would shift away from Europe. But the somewhat paranoid antics of European imperialism in decline should not prevent an acknowledgement that this decline was the result of a more general and profound European success. It was not just that European achievements in industrialisation provided a universal model for rapid and continuing wealth-creation, although this was immensely important. Perhaps even more significant was the world-wide export of European culture. To be sure, this has not been a one-sided transfer and other ancient cultures have not been destroyed by that of Europe. But the pervasiveness of European influence is apparent in such widely different forms as Indian films, Chinese urban hygiene, and South American football. More substantially, it is shown in the virtually universal adoption of forms of manufacturing industry, civil administration and military organisation which originated in Europe, and in the widespread use of European models for legal systems and representative institutions. European languages dominate the commercial and financial organisations of the world, as they do world transport systems and international communications.

The ending of European ascendancy and the generalisation of European cultural influence combine to make a reassessment necessary in the basic definition of our civilisation. Hitherto we have referred to it as 'Western Civilisation', with its convenient implication of a Western European origin. But the very successes of Western Civilisation in expanding its influence and riding the wave of the Promethean Revolution have converted it into a world civilisation for which the descriptive word 'Western' is now no longer appropriate, in whatever sense it is used. Our civilisation will henceforth be referred to as 'Industrial Civilisation', which carries a wider yet more explicit connotation than the previous description. It is, of course, linked to Western Civilisation by innumerable bonds and continuities. But in describing it in the context of the twentieth century – and in projecting its possible course of evolution in the coming centuries – it will be more realistic and accurate if we see ourselves as members of Industrial Civilisation.

8. *The Twentieth-century World*

Modern Industrial Civilisation emerged in a recognisable form in the twentieth century. Its origins, as we have seen, go back deep into the history of Western Civilisation and of the civilisations which preceded that, and it is the achievements of these earlier societies which have made our civilisation what it is. Without the Greek intellect and Hebrew individualism; without Roman administration and law; without the influences of Christianity, science, and technology; and without the experiences of expansion to world supremacy and of rapid industrialisation, the world today would be a very different place from that with which we are familiar, because Industrial Civilisation has combined all these factors and channelled them into a single, dynamic, world community. It is, therefore, not possible to arrive at even a reasonably comprehensive understanding of the contemporary world without grasping the significance of these historical forces which have framed it. Such an understanding, although indispensable, is only a beginning, and the hardest part of the analysis lies ahead. Scholars have long been aware of the perils of 'contemporary history', dealing with that penumbra zone of the immediate past from which prejudices and passions survive with undiminished vigour, but for which it has not yet been possible to make an objective assessment of the documentary evidence, so that it falls into a no-man's-land between the historian and the sociologist. Nevertheless, the recognition of our civilisation as a distinctively twentieth-century phenomenon, and the realisation that this civilisation is now confronted by some quite extraordinary problems, compels us to venture upon this treacherous ground. We will begin with the most obvious political realignments which have taken place in the twentieth century, and proceed then to consider the more elusive ideological changes and the evolution of expectations and aspirations.

The World at War

The historian of future centuries – if we may beg for the moment the question of whether any civilisation is likely to survive into future centuries – will probably look back on the first half of the twentieth century as one of virtually continuous international conflict between the same group of nation states. For thirty-one years from 1914, when war broke out between Germany on the one side, and France, Britain, and Russia, on the other, to 1945, when Germany was defeated and divided by the allies, at that time joined by the United States, there was a continuing condition of international tension only partially mitigated by the Versailles settlements after the first round of hostilities. This struggle had been anticipated by the Franco-Prussian War of 1870, because it inaugurated a new era of bitter rivalry between the two leading powers in continental Europe and initiated a change of attitude in British policy which was to transform the traditional rivalry with France into a military alliance. It thus began as a European conflict, but the rivalry of the European states throughout the world served to embroil most nations in a way which made it possible, for the first time in history, to speak of a 'World War'.

The outbreak of hostilities in 1914 was no more inevitable than any other historical event, but it had been made increasingly likely by the ostentatious display of national power by Germany, now firmly united under Prussian leadership, and by the antagonism engendered by this display in France, still smarting over its humiliation of 1870 and the loss of Alsace and Lorraine, and in Britain, where the growth of German naval strength and imperial pretensions had been viewed with apprehension amounting to alarm over the previous decade. Europe by 1914 had become a veritable tinder-box, and there was no shortage of sparks to ignite the charge. The details of the national alignments, however, were uncertain until the last moment, and were then resolved by the circumstances of a Balkan incident which caused Austria to issue an ultimatum against Serbia, and Russia to mobilise its army in defence of Serbia. Germany, coming to the defence of Austria, determined on a swift blow against Russia before its mobilisation could be completed, and declared war on both Russia and its ally, France. The German High Command had devised a plan – the Schlieffen Plan – for striking at France through its undefended frontier with Belgium, and promptly put this into action by moving against neutral Belgium. It was this act of aggression which finally persuaded the British government and public opinion to commit itself to the war, against Germany and in alliance with France. So the lines of European combat were drawn up.[1]

Germany possessed two considerable advantages over its opponents in 1914. It was the nation best prepared for war, with a highly industrialised economy and a well equipped army; and even though it was committed to a war on two fronts it had the advantage of interior lines of communication. The latter point was of great importance in the hey-day of the railway age, with Germany having an excellent network of railway services which could be used for moving men and supplies swiftly to whichever part of the frontier they were most required. The alliance against Germany, on the other hand, was a hotch-potch of nations which had difficulty in overcoming suspicions of one another's motives and, as far as attitudes to Russia were concerned, dislike of its internal political system. But behind the allied powers were the huge resources of the British and French empires and the possibility that the United States might be drawn into the conflict in support of world democracy. In the event, it was these resources which tipped the balance against Germany. The European powers fought themselves to a horrifying stalemate in the mud of trench warfare on the Western Front, but even the series of brilliant military victories of Germany on the Eastern Front which gave the Bolsheviks their long-awaited chance to seize power in Russia and to make a hurried settlement with Germany, could not avail against the increment of men, material, and perhaps most important of all, morale, once America threw its support behind the Western Allies. Although the German armies which had been victorious against Russia were moved swiftly across Europe to try one last offensive at the beginning of 1918, it was already too late and the impetus was soon lost. American entry assured German defeat in the long war of attrition in Flanders.

American commitment to the fighting was far from being a foregone conclusion in 1914. Apart from some residual suspicion towards Britain, there was considerable sympathy for Germany at the outbreak of the war, and a general feeling that the United States should not dabble in European politics. It had been one of the principles of the Fathers of the American Constitution that the United States should avoid embroilment in world power struggles, and with a continent to conquer, colonise, and govern, this was a rule adhered to for over a century by American political leaders. But as the frontier of settlement rolled westwards, new states were formed and incorporated into the union, floods of new immigrants came over from Europe, and the attitude towards Europe underwent a slow but subtle modification. This change of attitude was further promoted by the rapid spread of industrialisation in the United States, especially after the Civil War which, albeit at great cost, removed the internal conflict over slavery and preserved the union. America thus entered the twentieth century as a powerful, united, industrial nation, which was already challenging the world dominance of Europe and was searching to find a role for itself in the concert of nations. This challenge affected the economic and imperial interests of Britain and France as well as those of Germany, so that despite the similarity of democratic institutions between America and the Western Allies it could not be taken for granted that they would receive American support in the European war. It was the aggressive German attempt to impose an Atlantic blockade through submarine attacks on merchant ships that swung American opinion in favour of the Allies, and brought about the direct intervention of an American army on the Western Front. At a point when the other participants were close to exhaustion, this intervention was decisive and brought the German surrender in 1918.

The end of hostilities and the subsequent treaties signed at Versailles in 1919 did not bring stability to an unsettled world, and twenty years later the rivalries which had continued to smoulder ignited into open war again. There were several reasons for this. In the first place, the treaties sought to punish rather than to pacify: Germany was to be made to pay for her criminal aggression by the imposition of 'reparations', and the maintenance of these caused lasting bitterness in Germany and hindered the general economic recovery of Europe from the war. Secondly, the principle of national self-determination was enunciated at Versailles and applied to the corpses of the great European empires of Austria–Hungary, Russia, and Turkey. The result was a plethora of new nation states, mostly ill-conceived and lacking political experience, which presented abundant causes of dissension and rivalry amongst the older European powers. And thirdly, two key nations were not included in the Versailles settlement. The United States which, under President Wilson, had played such an important part in the outcome of the war, retreated after it into a phase of 'isolationism'. President Wilson was responsible for such idealism as was present at the Versailles conferences, and it was at his insistence that the League of Nations was created. But the American Senate refused to ratify the treaties, and swept along by a revulsion against European entanglements and a conviction that 'the business of the United States is business', the American government was unable to take an active part in international affairs. Isolationism was, if anything, reinforced by the great depression of the 1930s, so that the United States remained effectively outside world political affairs until Pearl Harbour in December 1941. The other great power left out of account in the Versailles settlement was Soviet Russia. The fragile régime of the Bolsheviks had made its own peace with Germany, but then had to struggle for several years against internal factions and external foes. Under Lenin, the ruthless programme of socialisation began in a nation which was still predominantly rural, and involved rapid industrialisation, the collectivisation of agriculture, the development of power resources and transport systems, and the relocation of labour. Stalin pursued these policies with paranoid intensity, eliminating opposition and potential rivals to his own authority to create a dictatorship of unprecedented scope. As far as world politics were concerned, however, his policy of 'socialism in one country' kept Russia very much on the side-lines, although not unwilling to support revolutionary activities in other countries provided this could be done without direct involvement. For Russia, as for America, the end of this phase came in 1941, when Hitler tore up his treaty of 1938 with Stalin and invaded the country.

The failure of the Versailles treaties to pacify Europe quickly became apparent in the years following 1919. Bitterness, frustration, and economic chaos combined to produce conditions in which well-organised groups of thugs were able to seize political power, first in Italy and then in Germany. The successes of Mussolini and Hitler derived from the experience of Versailles and caused the resumption of hostilities: their careers demonstrate the continuity of the Thirty-One Years War, even though Italy changed sides in the course of the respite from hostilities. Thus, when fighting resumed in 1939, the participants were essentially the same: Germany and its allies against France and Britain, with Russia and America joining them two years later. Economic depression and political inepititude had demoralised France and Britain in the 1930s, leaving them ill equipped to wage a major war at the end of the decade. But the revival of aggressive nationalism in Germany could not be indefinitely ignored, and after failing to respond to several militarist challenges, both countries made Hitler's invasion of Poland the pretext for declaring war. Hitler, however, was then well launched upon his expansionist policy, and an up-dated version of the Schlieffen Plan, relying this time on highly mobile armoured columns, secured the complete victory in the Low Countries and France which had eluded the German armies in 1914–18. Encouraged by his sweeping successes in 1940, Hitler turned in 1941 against his putative 'ally', Soviet Russia, and at the end of that year the attack of Japan against Pearl Harbour brought America into the World War and opened up a vast new theatre of military operations in the Pacific Ocean. These events completed the alignment of Germany, Italy, and Japan versus France (Free France persisted as a fighting force throughout the occupation), Britain, Russia, and the United States. They also brought the turn of the tide as far as the fortunes of war were concerned, because it became evident in 1942 and 1943 that both Germany and Japan had over-extended their resources, while the steady build-up of the power of the Allies made it increasingly doubtful whether any of their territorial gains could be held. In the event, the commitment of the Allies to the objective of unconditional surrender brought the complete collapse of the Axis powers, the dismemberment of Germany, and the explosion of the first atomic bombs in the summer of 1945. Whatever happened after the war, it was certain that the international scene would never be the same again.

In a formal sense, the Thirty-One Years War never came to a clear-cut end. Unlike the attempts at settlement in 1919 after the first round of hostilities, there were no general peace treaties in 1945 or thereafter. The Allies were able to dictate the terms of their occupation of the defeated nations, and peace treaties followed in a piece-meal way over the subsequent decades. What did happen after 1945, making the conventional sort of settlement obsolete, was that a fundamental realignment became apparent in world politics, and the focal point of world conflict passed decisively from the Western European context which had provided the cockpit of the previous alignment. There were two outstanding features in the new align-ment. One was the emergence of the United States and Soviet Russia as the dominant world powers, and the rivalry between them. This rivalry generated the so-called 'Cold War', divided Europe with the

'Iron Curtain' of Churchillian rhetoric, and was the source of a series of localised conflicts such as the wars in Korea and Vietnam. There have been various cross-currents in this rivalry, of which the most important has been the ambivalent role of China. Emerging in 1949 as a strong nation state uniting mainland China, it seemed inevitable that the Peoples' Republic of Mao Tse-tung would join Russia to reinforce the 'communist block' in world politics. But this relationship soon fell victim to nationalistic rivalries between Russia and China, so that the communist alliance broke down and China has become the single, greatest, imponderable factor in world politics.

The other new feature of the post-1945 world power alignment has been the development of a category of 'Third World' nations, standing apart from the main international tension between the United States and the Soviet Union but exercising an increasingly vocal influence in the world. The nations in this category are not European, because Europe has been almost completely divided between the supporters of the two great powers, illustrating vividly the way in which Europe has been converted from the centre of world interest to one of the many areas of peripheral concern. Most of the 'Third World' nations are new states, created largely from the breakdown of the old colonial empires of the European powers, and particularly the empires of Britain, France, and Holland. Others are states such as those of South America which were formed out of the ruins of the Spanish empire in the nineteenth century, but which have only recently begun to exercise any influence beyond that continent. Thus, in south-east Asia, in Africa, and in South America, there has appeared a formidable array of nation states which learnt their nationalism and much of their administrative and legal practice from Europe, but which reject European colonialism in all its forms, real or imagined. In some cases, such as India and the West African States, they appeal to ancient indigenous cultures and civilisations, but in all cases the common spiritual theme of their aspirations is the adoption of the belief in material progress demonstrated so effectively by Western Civilisation. The influence of these 'Third World' nations has to be reckoned with in the councils of world politics, at the United Nations and elsewhere. Their hostility or support is of great potential significance in the post-1945 power alignment. But it is necessary to remember that they are not an extraneous force in world politics. As much as the major powers, or the now-secondary powers of Europe, the new nations are a product of and an integral part of Industrial Civilisation.

Ideology and Idealism

The description just offered, admittedly much compressed and curtailed, of the changing alignments of national power in the course of the twentieth century, has given little attention to differences of ideology. It has not been possible to avoid them entirely, because ideological labels have become so closely associated with certain nations, but the attempt to minimise these contentions has been deliberate. Ideology has become one of the dangerous illusions of the modern world. Not necessarily because the contrasts it implies are wrong, but because emphasis on these contrasts has been used to obscure more fundamental differences. There are, of course, many differences of attitude and motivation amongst the policy-makers of the world, as there have always been, and for some purposes the degree of conviction involved in these points of view may be sufficiently strong to make it worth describing them as 'ideologies'. The universalist ideology of medieval Christendom has dwindled virtually to vanishing point, and with it has declined the ideology of a pan-Christian Empire and – less completely – the ideology of the embattled religious minority maintaining its integrity against the oppression of the majority.

Modern ideologies have tended to begin from secular, materialist assumptions, and have then polarised around different attitudes to the state and the individual. Liberals and democrats have normally adopted an ideology of individual freedom, while others have committed themselves to ideologies involving more initiative by the state. In the twentieth century, the latter have been represented by both fascists and communists. 'Fascism' has been allowed to become a general term of abuse, which is absurd as it has a specific historical connotation outside which it is strictly irrelevant. That historical situation was Italy from 1920–1945, when Benito Mussolini was able to impose his personal brand of dictatorship by state control, representing it as the apotheosis of brotherly comradeship bound together in the powerful image of the *fasces* which are individually weak but collectively strong. Contemporary with this, Hitler's National Socialism imposed a similar ideology on Germany, but added elements of racialism and anti-semitism which made it particularly repugnant to liberals. Communism resembles fascism and national socialism in its emphasis on centralised state control, but differs from them in the way in which it adopted this emphasis. There is considerable irony in the fact that Marx predicted the withering away of the state in his anticipated proletarian revolution, whereas the fulfilment of this revolution in Soviet Russia and elsewhere has led in every case to the strengthening of the centralised power of the state. Admittedly the doctrine has incorporated modifications in order to explain this paradox. In particular, Lenin's interpretation of the role of the organised *élite* in the Communist Party as the 'spearhead of the revolution', and the conception of the 'dictatorship of the proletariat', have provided convenient ideological justification for maintaining the power of the state. But essentially the state remains transitional in communist ideology, unlike that of fascism in which the state is an integral feature, even though the process of transition to a stateless paradise can be dismissed to the indefinite future.

From a liberal point of view, the conditions of life under all these modern state-orientated ideologies are indistinguishable and equally deplorable. In all of them, the individual is subordinated to the state in his political aspects, and in some his whole personality is liable to be sacrificed to the collective good as interpreted by the organs of the state. The alternative ideologies of liberalism have been represented in the twentieth century by the democratic political parties of Western Europe, North America, and elsewhere. They have been hampered by difficult economic conditions and the virulence of the state-promoting ideologies, and despite the moral victory shared by western democracies in 1945 they have adopted a largely defensive attitude against the world-wide expansion of communism. This defensiveness derives in part from the success of communist propaganda in identifying liberalism with capitalism and in making the latter one of the bogey-words of modern political vocabulary. A similar identification, even more meaningless and harmful, is constantly being suggested between liberalism and that other bogey-word, 'fascism'. However spurious these charges, there can be little doubt that they are made to sound plausible to many of the politically unsophisticated masses of the world. An even more serious cause of the defensive posture of liberalism is the fact that since 1939 all democratic political parties have been compelled to accept an increasing amount of state intervention in the life of the individual. It was necessary, in the first place, in order to win the war. It then became necessary in order to maintain economic control in a situation dominated by expensive scientific and technological operations. It has remained necessary to the present day because the complexity of modern society is such that it would cease to function without central state control. Thus liberals have been compelled to acknowledge the pressing claims of the state on the individual, and although there is no need to jump to the conclusion that individualism must be abandoned, the experience of trying to hold a balance between the state and the individual has been exhausting and, to a degree, demoralising.

If the ideological polarisation between the state and the individual can be abstracted from the confusion of the political forum and party propaganda, it becomes apparent that the contrast is generally overstated. In fact, neither absolute position is tenable, because even the most centralised state must take some account of the reaction of individuals, and the most liberal constitution must recognise the need for a strong state. As liberals have largely come to terms with the requirements of the twentieth-century state, a corresponding recognition by communist and other state-oriented ideologies of a Bill of Human Rights would serve to show the narrowness of the ideological gap. Such an abstraction from the arena of controversy is difficult, however, precisely because the ideological element has become entangled in a more fundamental conflict. It is in this sense that ideology has become a dangerous illusion, for it obscures this deeper conflict and generates controversy on matters which are often meaningless and at best pointless. The real conflict in the twentieth-century world, for which the ideological word-play provides an effective mask, is between rival nation states pursuing courses of national self-interest as they have done for the last 500 years in a world society which, in terms of international controls, still resembles a jungle with every nation fighting for itself, according to the free-for-all precept that might is right. The historical accident that Russia has adopted a communist ideology has not altered significantly the role of earlier Tsarist Russia in world affairs, although it has arguably made her more efficient in pursuing it. Although lacking the depth of historical precedent, the role of the United States in the modern world is equally one which has been dictated by the logistics of national self interest rather than by any ideological commitment to 'capitalism' or the 'free world'. The utter fatuity of the view that it is *ideologies* which separate the nations of the world is demonstrated by the conflict between communist Russia and communist China: where ideology should have cemented eternal friendship, traditional national rivalries along with a shared frontier and the clash of national interests in sensitive political areas of the world, have brought these giant nation states into sharp conflict.

The ultimate irony of the twentieth-century world is that despite all its vast scientific and technological competence it has so far failed to modify the basic instability of a world community in which every nation state jealously maintains its freedom to do as it will with its own. The extreme *laissez-faire* liberalism of those nineteenth-century western industrialists who claimed the right to use their resources as they wished without any interference from the state has long since been abandoned with the recognition by liberals that a strong state is an indispensable instrument of individual freedom. But the attitude persists in international relations, where the assertion of complete sovereignty by every nation state is accepted universally as the normal condition of affairs. The absurdity of this situation would have become apparent long since but for the confusion perpetrated in international discussion by the chimera of ideological conflict. As it is, there have been several attempts to secure greater harmony between nation states, if not to subdue their independent sovereignty. These attempts at internationalism, although so far unsuccessful, deserve our attention as important twentieth-century political developments, and potentially the most significant.

The need to reconcile conflicting sovereignties arose with the nation states themselves, as sixteenth-century rulers strove to establish alliances through treaty commitments and to guarantee national interests such as trade on the high seas. A body of 'international law' thus developed, although the title 'law' is inappropriate for a set of rules which had no authority other than the goodwill of the nations accepting them and no sanctions other than the withdrawal of such limited convenience as the law could offer. Nevertheless, amongst a community of nations sharing many common interests, the convenience of this arrangement was sufficient to make it necessary, even though every state reserved the right to break such international laws as it thought fit. The Dutch jurist Hugo Grotius first worked out the principles of international law in his *De Jure Belli et Pacis* at the beginning of the seventeenth century, and these were gradually enlarged and filled in by the experience of conducting relationships between sovereign states over succeeding centuries. Trade, the treatment of foreign nationals, the observance of treaty agreements, the conduct of war, and behaviour towards prisoners of war, were all brought within the area of agreed custom and practice which passed in Europe as international law down to the twentieth century. The cataclysmic experience of the 1914–18 hostilities, however, put the combatants into a sober frame of mind in which they were prepared to consider ways of preventing a recurrence of such horrors. In this frame of mind, President Wilson was able to present his idealistic notion of a League of Nations, and the strength of the United States at the conference tables of 1919 was such that support for the League was written into the various peace treaties of that year.

For all the idealism of its inspiration, the League of Nations was a modest body. It did not attempt to encroach on the sovereignty of its member states, and although it established a splendid palace for itself at Geneva, it was never much more than an international forum where the member states could meet regularly to confer about common problems and to recommend action by members when it was considered appropriate to do so. The idealistic and essentially noble aspect of this specification was the belief that it was only necessary to get the nations of the world to talk together in order to prevent conflict. But however idealistic and noble, it was also unrealistic, as quickly became apparent when the United States refused to ratify the 1919 treaties and consequently never joined the League. The League, indeed, never recovered from its uncertain start. It performed well its intended function as an international forum, but it was evident from the beginning that no member state would be prepared to agree to a League decision which was contrary to its own national interest, and as soon as such self-interests became aggressive once more, led by Japan, Italy, and Germany, the League lost even the semblance of authority which it had acquired by virtue of being a talking shop. With the world collapsing into a resumption of hostilities in 1939, the League came effectively to an end. Yet it cannot be said to have failed: the little that could be done by international discussion and agreement was done. What failed was the will of its members to make the League succeed.

However discouraging the record of the League of Nations in maintaining international harmony may have appeared in 1939, it had demonstrated the need of the twentieth-century world for an international body through which the states of the world could resolve their differences. Thus the demise of the League led directly to plans for its successor, and while the war was still in progress representatives of the Allies met in 1944 to establish the United Nations Organisation. Learning at least some lessons from the fate of the League, the constitution of the United Nations Organisation (UN) was ingeniously constructed to give the great powers more influence – including a veto – over policy-making through making them permanent members of the Security Council, while the General Assembly became the major forum for airing grievances. The UN, moreover, was equipped with impressive headquarters in New York and a strong secretariat presided over by a General Secretary who has been recognised as a major world statesman even though he wields no sovereign power. As the head of important international agencies such as the World Health Organisation (WHO), the General Secretary of the UN is able to assert substantial administrative influence.

The scenario created for the UN after the ending of the war was thus one of considerably more prospective influence than that enjoyed by the League of Nations. Its deliberations were taken very seriously in a war-weary world, and although there were many frustrations caused by the Russian use of its veto powers, the agencies established by the Organisation achieved some very significant successes in improving standards of life, and when international conflict threatened in 1950 the UN was able to send a force into South Korea and to reassert the *status quo*. It must be admitted that the intervention in the Korean War was an accident, as it was only made possible by the temporary withdrawal of the Soviet Union (as a protest – ironical in view of their future conflict – against the exclusion of the new Peoples' Republic of China). But it set a pattern of UN-led international peace-keeping forces which was used later to good effect in the Congo, Cyprus, and elsewhere when threats of international tension could be considered without one or other of the Security Council powers exercising its veto. This condition, however, was not fulfilled when a great power saw its own interests affected by a dispute, so that the powers of intervention available to the UN are severely limited. In one vital respect the UN is no stronger than the League: no member state is required to make any concession of its sovereignty, and thus retains complete power (subject only to the law of the international jungle) to do anything it chooses to do.

Even though world power-alignments have changed dramatically since the beginning of the twentieth century, the condition of world politics remains fundamentally unchanged with the nation state as the indivisible unit, each state preserving its autonomy. The idealism expressed in the liberal hope that nationalism would lead by easy stages into internationalism has not been fulfilled, and the international organisations which have anticipated the emergence of a genuine sense of internationalism have either foundered on the rock of militant nationalism like the League of Nations, or adapted themselves to a more diminished role than that expressed by their founders, like the United Nations Organisation. Yet in a century which has demonstrated forcibly the moral bankruptcy of nationalism and the inability of nation states to preserve international stability, the UN remains the only signpost to possible improvement. It may be idealistic to state one's faith in such a rudimentary international organisation. But there is no sign of an acceptable alternative.

Technology Comes of Age

One of the momentous developments of the twentieth century has been the greatly increased social influence of science and technology. As we have seen, the scientific revolution and its practical application in technology played a vital part in the expanding processes of wealth creation and of industrialisation. Until the middle of the nineteenth century there was little attempt made to distinguish between science, which was understood as 'natural philosophy' involving the attempt to achieve systematic knowledge of all aspects of man and his environment, and technology, which meant simply the study of arts and crafts. Although it is possible to discern an incipient social distinction between the 'gentlemen scientists' of the period and the 'unlettered artisans' who were the main practitioners of technology, it is unrealistic to emphasise it because there was a great deal of flexibility about the distinction and a more accurate appraisal of the situation would stress the common endeavour to find practical applications for new knowledge. This was the Baconian tradition in British science at least, and it found its most tangible expression in the groups of provincial industrialists with a penchant for natural philosophy of which the 'Lunar Society' of Birmingham was the outstanding example, but by no means untypical of the world-changing mentality which characterised the exponents of rapid industrialisation.[2] In a sense, this unity of science and technology, of thought and practice, was undermined by its own success, because with the spread of sophisticated techniques in industry and transport systems, in means of communication and administrative organisation, the demand for evermore specialised skill promoted the distinction not only between science and technology, but between the various sciences and technologies. It was no longer feasible for any one scientist to be a master of the whole range of natural sciences, or for an engineer to be both an outstanding bridge designer and a mechanical expert. Each branch of knowledge and each skill acquired its own expertise, its own training programme, and its own institutional representation. With success, therefore, came fragmentation, and the derivative problems of social distinctions and status.

This process of fragmentation was well advanced in Britain by the end of the nineteenth century. But it remained a fairly small-scale matter, involving a relatively small proportion of the population and a negligible amount of public funds. Science, although well regarded and accepted as an academic discipline, was still a small-scale operation carried out by devoted men and women in poorly equipped laboratories and with a minimum of financial resources. Some French and German scientists had better facilities, because in these countries the practical application of science to exciting new developments in bacteriology, the chemical industry, and the electrical industry, were already being recognised. For the most part, however, science was still definitely a minority preoccupation, and the transformation of this 'little science' into the 'big science' with which we have become familiar in the modern world has only been accomplished in the twentieth century.[3] The transformation has sprung from a recognition of the indispensability of large-scale science and technology to both military survival and to peace-time prosperity. Occurring in the context of international conflict and rivalry which we have described, this meant that every nation-state capable of investing resources in science and technology has done so, and has continued to do so in order to keep its position in relation to its rivals. Some aspects of this rivalry are harmless enough, but others are supremely dangerous. In particular, the commitments of huge scientific and technological resources to the arms race pose a threat of potentially catastrophic proportions to the whole world. The transformation in the scale of science and technology is thus one of great importance, and it is necessary to explain how it came about.

In the first place, the build-up was a direct continuation of developments which had already begun in the nineteenth century with the growth of 'science-based' industries. All industries, it may be claimed, have some scientific content, but what was new about these late nineteenth-century industries was that they would not have occurred at all without major scientific discoveries. These took place in precisely those fields in which we have just observed continental nations placing significant resources: in chemical processes, electrical engineering, pharmaceutics, and so on. The new artificial dyes, high explosives, artificial fibres and plastics industries, were all chemical processes derived from basic scientific research in organic chemistry. Similarly, the manufacture of electricity-generating dynamoes and of electrical motors in a rapidly widening variety of applications, was a result of scientific research into the nature and characteristics of electrical energy. It is thus reasonable to describe these as 'science-based' industries. Their importance was already clear at the beginning of the twentieth century, but the demands of the 1914–1918 war for the products of such industries justified its description as a 'chemist's war'.[4] The rapid advances in the petro-chemical industry have ensured the continued growth of the chemical industries, with crude oil providing the raw material for innumerable everyday necessities of modern life.

While these industries developing out of the nineteenth-century scientific research have grown from strength to strength, another huge range of industrial exploitation has followed on scientific discoveries in atomic physics which only began to make significant progress at the turn of the century. Modern physics has undergone its own scientific revolution in the twentieth century, as a result of the discovery of the electron and radioactivity, a new understanding of the structure of the atom, and the fundamental conceptual changes springing from Einstein's theory of relativity. The industrial applications of this revolution swiftly became apparent in radio and in communications technology generally. The longer-range applications, of even more epoch-making quality, emerged with the scientific achievement of nuclear fission and the detonation of the first atomic bomb in 1945. If World War I can be described as a 'chemist's war', it is equally fair to describe World War II as a 'physicist's war', for in addition to the work on the 'Manhattan Project' which led to the production of the atomic bomb, physics played a vital part in the war through radar and other electronic devices.[5] Through these and other scientific applications such as the manufacture of antibiotics for wartime medicine and of nylon for parachute cord, science and technology demonstrated their indispensability for the war effort, and ever since 1945 it has been impossible for any nation wishing to keep its position in relation to its rivals to neglect investment in these areas.

But it is not only in war that modern Industrial Civilisation has accepted its dependence upon large-scale science and technology. Where war-needs promoted the manufacture of penicillin, subsequent pharmaceutical advances in antibiotics and related fields have received substantial support. Where war, likewise, stimulated the development of insecticides such as DDT, the post-war chemical industry has been able to exploit a huge market for insecticides, herbicides, fertilisers, and other synthetic materials derived from current scientific research. And where war demonstrated the value of new electronic techniques, the post-war world has gone on to create an apparently limitless range of applications for the products of this branch of physics. Electronics, indeed, has been one of the fastest growing modern industries, with a remarkable succession of basic scientific discoveries constantly transforming the technological applications in hardware such as television sets and electronic computers. The ubiquitous computer, with its ability to perform rapidly calculations which would have been inconceivable before, has become one of the most potent symbols of the modern world, and the television-set has become an essential feature of every home in the advanced industrial nations. In peace as in war, modern society has come to rely completely on the performance of science and technology. The occasional error has not affected this dependence: the tragedy of thalidomide, and the frightening pollution by DDT and other toxic substances, have been accepted as part of the price to be paid for dependence, and to be contained as well as possible. The modern world is committed to high levels of investment in science and technology, which includes the training of large labour forces and the equipment of major research facilities as well as industrial production. In this situation, it may be said without exaggeration that technology has come of age, for it is on the technological hardware produced by the application of scientific discoveries that the dependence of the modern world is most apparent. For good or ill, 'Big Science' – which subsumes technology – has come to stay.

Some commentators have suggested that technology has not merely come to stay, but that it has taken over modern society completely. According to this view, we are now so utterly dependent on the support of technology that we could not survive without it: we have become slaves to a soulless repetitive machine technology both in our work and in our leisure, and in this situation it has become impossible to express oneself with meaningful individuality because all important decisions are taken either by an electronic computer or by an anonymous technocrat who, though nominally in charge of the machines, is as much in bondage to them as the rest of us.[6] This interpretation should not be lightly dismissed. There is certainly plenty of cause for anxiety about the debilitating effects of much modern work of a machine-serving character, and the tendency towards mass-production has greatly increased this sort of work. Moreover, it may be conceded that technology acquires a quality of self-sustaining momentum in its impact on society which is potentially dangerous. The very scale of investment required to set up a new productive plant ensures that political and social commitments must be made in order to give it an opportunity to demonstrate its value in terms of commercial profit or social advantage. These decisions then prejudice later choices, and thus 'technological momentum' comes to assume the force of an impersonal compulsion. Alternatively, but equally harmful to the processes of democratic decision-making, the major choices frequently involve technological judgements of such complexity that only the experts are able to make them, so that there is a tendency to abdicate in favour of the technocrats who are recognised as possessing the necessary competence.

The dangers of both technological momentum and technocracy are real enough, but there is no need to accept them as inevitable conditions of modern Industrial Civilisation about which nothing can be done. Their main danger, indeed is that they further sap the weakened nerve of liberal individualism, because the main chance of keeping technology under control is the determination of individuals so to retain control. The pessimistic view that individuals are already too far gone in being conditioned to reliance on machines ever again to assert their independence of technology may, in the event, prove to have been right. But to admit this would be to throw in the metaphorical towel and thus help it to become a self-fulfilling prophecy, with disastrous consequences. It is infinitely preferable to face the future of technological society with optimism, aware of all its dangers but grateful also for all its advantages and confident that appropriate political and administrative structures can be devised to maintain adequate control. Like so many of the problems of modern society, the answer lies largely in our ability to develop the sort of educational system which will enable the next generation of citizens to deal confidently with technology. In recognising that technology has come of age, therefore, it is necessary to accommodate it as a mature component of Industrial Civilisation, and to maintain it as a constructive and progressive force in our society.

The Era of Affluence

While the nation-state remains rampant in the twentieth century, and the moves towards internationalism are weak and ineffective, a change of great significance has taken place within the frontiers of the leading western states and has spread thence to influence all parts of the world either in actuality or in aspiration. This change may be described tersely as the advent of affluence. Ever since Professor Galbraith popularised the concept of 'the affluent society', it has received a lot of attention and criticism, so that it is necessary to use the term with some caution.[7] It should be observed, in the first place, that the word 'affluence' carries no necessary overtones of approval or of condemnation: it is a morally neutral term describing a material condition. As such it does not refer to conditions of the mind or of the spirit, which may be healthy or unhealthy, mature or barren, in conditions of material affluence as in any other. The other preliminary caution about the use of the term 'affluent society' is to stress that it can only properly be applied to the advanced industrial societies of Western Europe, North America, and elsewhere. It would be tasteless mockery to describe the lot of an oriental peasant in an over-populated and under-nourished community as in any sense 'affluent', although even in such under-developed or developing societies the prospect of material affluence is frequently seen as a vision and an object of aspiration. That, however, is another matter:

the immediate point is that the geographical scope of the 'affluent society' is severely limited.

Another striking fact about the experience of affluence is its novelty. Industrialisation, to be sure, has enormously increased the productive capacity of societies which have adopted it from the eighteenth century onwards, but until late in the nineteenth century most of this increased productivity was absorbed in coping with the needs of a rapidly growing population and such affluence as was achieved was the monopoly of the property-owning classes. For the mass of the people, in Britain and elsewhere, conditions of life remained arduous, with very long working hours, virtually no holidays, and a standard of living that was only marginally above subsistence level. Economic historians have had recently an interesting but not very illuminating controversy about the standard of living in Britain in the first half of the nineteenth century. Did it rise or fall? The fact that this could have been a cause of dispute shows that the change must have been minimal, one way or the other. What confuses the issue is the recognition that whatever change occurred or failed to occur in the *standard* of living, there was a clear change in the *conditions* of life as people moved into the new towns and factories. Whatever improvements in diet, in clothing, in housing and domestic utensils – and there were definite improvements in all these respects available to most families – they were enjoyed in conditions of urban squalor and factory discipline which destroyed any sense of euphoria or material affluence.[8]

Nor was there any dramatic development towards affluence in the second half of the nineteenth century. In Britain, the campaign to limit the prodigious hours of labour which were still normal for most working men, women, and children, began to bear some fruit. Marx had directed his inspired invective against the industrialists who had imposed these excessive hours in *Das Kapital*, published in 1867, but already as he wrote – thanks partly to his own efforts and those of other middle-class radicals as well as the growth of powerful trade unions – conditions were beginning to improve.[9] Hours of work were curtailed by factory legislation, by the imposition of compulsory primary education, and by the pressure of an increasingly vocal public opinion. Half-day holidays and statutory holidays were introduced, to be followed in the twentieth century by holidays with pay. The food available to the mass of the people increased in both quantity and quality, so that more money was spent on meat, fresh vegetables, and dairy produce. Luxuries such as chocolate, soap, and tobacco underwent a market boom, exploited for the first time by extensive advertising. In these and other respects, there were clear indications of rising living standards and expectations by the beginning of the twentieth century, but these could hardly have been described as 'affluence'. The gains had been too hard-bought and their possession was still too vulnerable to changes in the market or even to such routine catastrophes as growing old. Enjoyment of affluence presupposes a degree of security, and this was not yet assured.

The first half of the twentieth century saw in British politics a determined effort to establish such social security in the form of the 'welfare state'. Like the rest of the economic life of the nation, it was at the mercy of the international trade depression of the 1920s and 1930s, so that for many years little progress was made in the welfare legislation introduced by the Liberal administration from 1906 to 1914. But the coming of World War II provided an opportunity to rethink many domestic policies, and the Beveridge Report of 1941 set out a plan for comprehensive social security which was largely incorporated in the post-war programme of the Labour government. By this time, also, another vital lesson had been learnt in economic planning. Keynesian economics had demonstrated a positive function for government expenditure which made the budget-balancing emphasis of the traditional financial administrators appear old-fashioned. Instead, the state stepped in to promote investment and to abolish unemployment, which had been the biggest curse of the pre-war depression. Thus, with full employment apparently guaranteed indefinitely, and with basic standards of social security established, conditions were at last congenial to the enjoyment of affluence.

Of course we know that these conditions have no guarantee of permanence. The economic sophistications of Lord Keynes have, in the event, failed to maintain full employment in the leading industrial nations, and the welfare state has been proved to be less of the general panacea for the ills of society than its founders had believed. Some western nations, indeed, have kept welfare legislation to a minimum (in America the welfare state is regarded as a form of 'creeping socialism'), although they have all made some provision for the elderly, the sick, and the unemployed. The enjoyment of affluence has thus not been undisturbed by apprehensions that it may be only a transient phenomenon. But for a quarter of a century since

1950, the leading industrialised nations of the world have managed to maintain high living standards for their citizens, so that comparative material affluence has become a matter of every-day experience for most people for a generation. The effects of this are of profound importance for the prospects of Industrial Civilisation. They are also so complex and so involved with the contentions of modern politics that it is difficult for the historian to comment upon them without his judgement becoming impaired by partisan or moralistic considerations. Nevertheless, a few observations should be made.

In the first place, the experience of affluence has precipitated contemporary society into a condition of cultural shock. The experience, after all, is so novel that there is no clear precedent to guide behaviour in response to it. In the past, affluence has been enjoyed only by small minorities, who have sometimes flaunted it ostentatiously in the form of 'conspicuous consumption'[10] and at other times used it less obstrusively in improving their own estates, but in both cases it was taken for granted that affluence could purchase an army of servants and other minions. This does not apply when virtually everybody has a measure of affluence, so that domestic and personal service has been reduced to a minimum while the mechanical aids made available by modern technology have relieved men and women of many of the worst chores of repetitive labour in both industrial and domestic work. At the same time, a significant increase in leisure, the development of the mass media of entertainment, and means of rapid transport, have combined to place much more of the world and its cultural facilities at their disposal than would have been conceivable a mere two generations ago. Affluence, in short, has made available to the citizens of modern industrial society a completely new way of life, and the consequences of this novelty are bound to be disturbing for conventional assumptions about work, leisure, the family, and other social relationships.

As conditions of affluence are clearly preferable to the lack of affluence for most people, the maintenance of these conditions becomes a matter of supreme political importance. Not even the totalitarian régimes can afford to ignore the new-found affluence of their citizens, however limited it may be in terms of consumer goods compared with the western democracies, but with the democratic political parties the preservation of affluence is a *sine qua non* of survival. If a situation occurs in which it is no longer possible to maintain affluence, it is likely that present democratic institutions will be in peril. The rise in rates of unemployment in the industrialised nations over recent years is alarming, both for the direct suffering which it causes, and because it puts democracy at risk.

Another political consequence of affluence has been the change of meaning in traditional doctrines and distinctions based on pre-affluent conditions. Most significant in this respect is the class war of socialist dogma. The affluent society has not destroyed social differences, and in some ways it has accentuated them: the material possibilities of ostentatious living are now greater than they have ever been, so that the life-style of the rich is widely known. But in several ways affluence has brought a fundamental reorientation in class attitudes. For one thing, the common media of mass communication provide a shared experience which offsets the differences of group experiences. Secondly, the development of large-scale industry and other services with a high level of state participation has blurred beyond all recognition the traditional distinction, enshrined in left-wing dogma, between the expropriators and the expropriated. The 'managerial revolution', however it is interpreted, has introduced innumerable grades of responsibility in modern society which make the old black and white categories of the class war obsolete. By the same process the promise of flexibility, of movement upwards through the various levels of responsibility (and remuneration), is held out to everybody, however illusory it may be to many. And thirdly, the experience of affluence serves as a most effective damper on revolutionary ardour. If even those who are deemed to occupy lowly positions on the social ladder are conscious of the advantages of a steady income (good home, plenty of food, annual holidays, television, and so on), they are not likely to be interested in political policies designed to upset this equilibrium. It is no longer true that the mass of the working population have nothing to lose but their chains.

Affluence is also having important political repercussions through the modification of the educational system of advanced industrial societies. Education – primary, secondary, and tertiary – is now claimed as a right for every boy and girl, and this has been acknowledged as one of the foremost services which the welfare state provides for its citizens. It would be comforting to believe that in conditions of affluence there would be great pressure on the educational services to supply ever more comprehensive and versatile training for both young people and adults. Unfortunately, this does not appear to be the dominant trend. Instead, the prospect of comparatively easy money in routine employment draws too many young people away from education at too early an age, and the traditional structure of educational institutions has made it difficult to offer the sort of flexible courses which might be appreciated by young people who associate school with childhood and are anxious to leave it behind. There is thus a real danger of deterioration in the general educational services of industrial societies, even though the specialised education available to the minority increases in intensity. The affluent society could be the prelude to a semi-literate society, in which the dominant images are visual and aural, derived from the mass media rather than the printed word, and this is a prospect which should be deeply alarming to educationalists.

Prognostications such as these are admittedly speculative, and are based upon suggestive trends rather than upon rigorous analysis of all the available data. As such they illustrate in part the value of an historical awareness which can recognise trends in the evolution of modern society, but they also indicate the dangers of extrapolating such trends into a discussion of contemporary social problems. There is no lack of serious social problems in our Industrial Civilisation – disorientation and *anomie*, urban violence and sexual permissiveness, crime and vandalism to name but a few of the more obvious subjects of contemporary concern – and historical evidence is invaluable in the discussion of all of them. But they have all been the subjects of intensive study by politicians, administrators, and academic social scientists, so that it is impossible to do justice to any of them without devoting considerable time and space to their examination. From the point of view of the present study, therefore, we have probably gone as far as we can in indicating the outlines of the twentieth-century world and the particular problems created by the novel experience of affluence in modern industrial societies. The historian is well equipped to draw attention to this novelty, and to suggest aspects deserving more intensive study. He can also make an essential contribution to the detailed analysis of these aspects, but that can best be done in co-operation with other social scientists, working to achieve a perception in depth of each problem in turn. Perhaps, in doing so, the historian will manage to demonstrate that many of the problems beloved of the Sunday journalists are not as unprecedented and intractable as they are portrayed in some of the more lurid accounts. But on one thing, at least, the historical judgement will be unambiguous: the environment and society created by Industrial Civilisation in the twentieth century are, in many of their dominant aspects, strikingly novel. The world-wide power alignments of modern states, with their technological base giving them access to colossal power and making comparative affluence available to their citizens, are features unique to the present century. However thoroughly we search the records for precursors and anticipations, and however much we insist that the twentieth-century world is the product of many centuries of historical development, our conclusion must be that contemporary Industrial Civilisation is unique.

9. The Lessons of History

It has frequently been said, both cynically and sadly, that the only thing we learn from history is that we learn nothing from history. In the sense that a knowledge of history cannot necessarily avert an impending disaster, and may even help to precipitate it, there is undoubtedly some substance in the dictum. Thus, Adolf Hitler was unable to defy the climatic logistics which had defeated Napoleon's invasion of Russia, even though he was well aware of them. And western politicians in the mid-1950s, imbued with a strong historical sense, identified President Nasser of Egypt with the career of Hitler and undertook a catastrophic military operation on the strength of this misjudgement of history. Yet in these as in all similar cases, disaster should only be attributed to a failure to learn from history if the careers of innumerable successful constitution-makers and empire-builders are set in the opposite balance as examples of people who did manage to read aright the signs of their times. History, after all, represents a vast fund of available knowledge, from which either wisdom or misconception may be distilled. What is certain is that anybody who refuses to try to learn from history is risking fatuity of mind and intellectual sterility. Knowledge of our past is the single greatest resource available to man, and whether we use this asset well or badly, we neglect it at our peril. It has been the purpose of this book to argue that our modern Industrial Civilisation is the product of the cumulative experience of many centuries of social evolution, and that the proper understanding of the present world and of its future prospects depends heavily upon an appreciation of this process of historical development. As an exercise in applied history, therefore, it is important to derive both general and particular lessons from the past in order to illuminate our understanding of contemporary society. That is the object of the present chapter, and in the next and final chapter we will attempt to project this understanding into a discussion of possible future developments.

Historical Interpretations

Logically, the first lessons which we learn from history are those concerned with the interpretation of history. We have to decide about the objectivity and subjectivity of historical experience. We have to decide whether or not 'general laws' exist in history. And if we decide that they do exist, we have to determine what they are and how they have dictated the pattern of historical evolution. These questions were touched upon briefly in the first chapter, but it is necessary to take them up again here in relation particularly to the problem of interpreting the development of Industrial Civilisation.

Historians of the late nineteenth century, who laid the foundations of the study of history as an academic discipline in the universities of Europe and North America, hoped to achieve an objective and complete recall of the past as it had actually happened, and many of them hoped thereby to reveal the 'positive' laws governing the historical process. In the fashionable relativism of the twentieth century, we have come to accept that such objectivity is never attainable, so that human history is not capable of being reduced to a few overriding principles or laws. It seems likely that this current attitude towards history is more than a fashionable trend, and represents a perception of the past which has examined the claims of historical objectivity and has found them inadequate beyond any hope of rehabilitation. The best modern understanding of history is that it is an interpretation of past experience mediated through the mind of the interpreter. The interpreter is responsible for making the selection of significant information from the vast repository of past events, and for presenting his selection in an intelligible manner in order to explain *how* and *why* things happened. Thus the emphasis has shifted from the aim of recovering *what* happened to recognising the vital role of the historian in the process of recovering an understanding of the past. In short, we now accept the inevitability of historical subjectivity, because everybody is able to make his or her own interpretation of the past on the basis of whatever primary or secondary evidence is available to them.

This recognition of the subjective element in the study of history in no way diminishes the scholarly task of searching out the best possible evidence in the reconstruction of historical explanations. On the contrary, it serves to reinforce the need for historical research because it starts from the admission that the task of the historian is never complete. In a real sense, every generation needs to rewrite its own history for the simple reason that the apprehension of the past by every human being is constantly changing in the light of that human being's own experience of life, and over a period of years the experience of individuals and of societies can undergo very significant modifications. History, therefore, is a highly dynamic study, undergoing perpetual change as the standpoint of the observer alters over time. Its material – our evidence of past events – requires constant reworking in order to test existing interpretations and to tease out explanations which make more sense in the circumstances of the present. Far from being the end of the study of history, the admission of subjectivity thus opens up an endless task of sorting and sifting the available material in order to produce interpretations which are more significant to the needs of the present.

If this view of the subjective element in our historical comprehension is accepted, it makes the issue of general 'laws' of history largely irrelevant. It may be maintained that history is subject to human 'laws' of birth and death, but this is not very helpful. History is largely concerned with human beings, but the natural conditions to which humans are subject do not constitute historical 'laws' in any meaningful sense. It would be more pertinent to claim that history tells us about human nature, and that this knowledge constitutes a series of 'laws'. But however valuable such knowledge may be – and we will return to the point shortly – it cannot be resolved into a set of simple propositions which will enable us to predict behaviour in any conceivable situation, which is what would be required of a 'law of history'. If such laws are sought in the matrix of historical events rather than in the nature of the human beings who participate in those events, we enter an intriguing world of 'meta-history'. It is intriguing because there would undoubtedly be great intellectual satisfaction in laying bare the grand principles – the 'laws' – of historical processes. Many historians in the past have been beguiled by this prospect and have devised systems of varying degrees of sophistication, purporting to explain the pattern of human history and to predict its outcome. Every religion and political philosophy has found it necessary to erect its own meta-history in order to justify its own claims in the present and anticipation for the future, but these interpretations may be regarded as special pleading and should not be taken too seriously. More to our point is the fact that some outstanding scholars have expounded meta-histories for which explanatory and predictive claims have been made. Three of these – the systems of Marx, Spengler, and Toynbee – deserve to be mentioned, although it is impossible to give them an extensive consideration here.

The role of Marxism in the transformation of industrial society has already been given some attention (see chapter 6). Here it is only necessary to comment on the acceptability of Marx's meta-historical views. Marx believed in historical laws – in particular, he believed in the dialectical evolution of social classes promoted by economic conditions, in such a way that human individuals could have little, if any, effect on the course of history, and the ends of the historical process were thus predetermined. This view of history has close affinities with the evolutionary habit of thinking which was fashionable in nineteenth-century Europe, represented by Hegel, who provided Marx with his 'dialectical' method, and by Charles Darwin, who developed his explanation of the evolution of species by natural selection. It was hardly surprising, therefore, that Marx was a warm admirer of Darwin, although the legend that he sought Darwin's permission to dedicate a book to him has been shown to be without documentary foundation. The elegance of Darwin's theory as applied to natural species was so great that it inspired many social scientists to seek a similar formula for human history. Marx did not incorporate 'natural selection' in his system, but it was nevertheless a profoundly evolutionary interpretation. More specifically, it made forecasts, and as any predictive system is open to a simple verification test of trial and error, Marx's account has failed. Despite all the attempts of Marxist scholars to explain why the predictions of the master have not been fulfilled, the indisputable historical fact is that events have not turned out as Marx predicted.

As few historical interpretations have ever possessed the monumental erudition with which Marx supported his system, it might have seemed that the manifest failure of this system to fulfil its predictions would have caused not only a collapse in the following which Marx's own system received but also a revulsion from meta-history in general. But far from it: the twentieth century has witnessed an enormous proliferation of Marxist exegesis as followers of Marx have explained to their own satisfaction the failures of the original thesis and introduced modifications to make it applicable in current circumstances; and followers of other doctrines have vied with the Marxists in promulgating their own meta-histories. Amongst historical scholars, the names of Spengler and Toynbee have been outstanding. Both of them approached the task of unveiling regularities in the patterns of history with the same sort of vast erudition which Marx had brought to the task. Their systems, though strikingly similar in determining on civilisations as their major units of historical analysis, are very different in their diagnosis and prognostications. Spengler took the sombre view that, as civilisations follow a 'natural' process of birth, growth, maturation, and decay, Western Civilisation was currently in decline (his book was published in 1918) and would shortly collapse. Toynbee, in developing his ideas over many years, was more cautious (or just vague) in his analysis of the internal dynamics of civilisations, and came to a more optimistic conclusion: his 'challenge and response' formula allowed an open-ended interpretation of history in which the future could always be modified by a change in the human response to the challenges confronting a civilisation at any particular time.[1]

These twentieth-century meta-histories are less easily faulted than that of Marx because sufficient time has not yet elapsed to demonstrate incontrovertibly the inaccuracy of their predictions. To be sure, Western Civilisation has shown rather more vitality in the last sixty years than Spengler attributed to it, but the possibility of decay and collapse along the sort of lines he envisaged cannot be dismissed as impossible or even as a remote possibility. As far as Toynbee's predictions are concerned, it may be considered that by the end of his long life he had so hedged his bets that any development could be incorporated within his system, which had thus lost any specific predictive quality. Even if the meta-history must remain, for some decades at least, beyond the reach of final criticism, the systems of both Spengler and Toynbee are open to severe criticism as history. While exercising the sort of selection which is inevitable in any historical scholarship, the tendentious bias of their selection to suit the theories they were expounding has come under review in many specific instances. Their tendency to elevate a speculative thesis into an objective observation in order to fit the requirements of their systems has also attracted critical attention. However stimulating their speculations may be to the modern reader, therefore, it is important that they should not be taken too seriously. The general laws of historical evolution which they expound are definitely not proven. Like all meta-histories, they carry ingenious speculation to the brink of credibility, and attempt to make predictions which are either incapable of being tested or which have been tested and found to be deficient.

One feature of all interpretations of history which purport to establish grand patterns and rhythms in the unfolding of the human drama is that they tend to become deterministic. That is to say, they lead to the conclusion that certain processes are operating which no human intervention can prevent. This applies equally to prophecies of Armageddon, the inevitability of class war, or the imminent collapse of civilisation. They maximise non-human forces, whether these be the gods, economic factors, or fate, and correspondingly minimise the contribution of human individuality. There may be good reasons for this emphasis, and surely no defender of individual initiative could deny that the non-human forces as well as the collective weight of all the other individual forces except his own greatly constrict the field of operation of human individuality. But in the past as in the present it is the individuals who are the most significant elements in human history, and thus to denigrate the importance of individualism is not just to attack an old-world, unfashionable, liberalism: it is to undermine the only meaningful basis for the study of history – the better understanding of our fellow human beings. This is the fact from which our interpretation of history should begin.

Human Nature in History

Once the search for general laws in history is abandoned, and the inevitable subjectivity of any historical interpretation is accepted, it becomes possible to reappraise the role of human nature in history. In place of the determinism which is implied, to a greater or lesser extent, in all meta-historical views of mankind, it is possible to assert a principle of indeterminateness as the prime lesson of historical understanding. According to this principle, history never repeats itself in any precise and meaningful sense, not only because life is a ceaseless flux of events undergoing constant change, but because the reactions of human beings are always unique and individual and therefore not predictable. It is true, as demographic historians and other scholars employing statistical techniques have succeeded in demonstrating, that large numbers of people tend to behave in certain ways in response to particular conditions, and very useful analyses may be performed on the basis of a knowledge of such conformities of behaviour to predict population trends, market possibilities, and electoral changes. It is largely on the strength of such aggregate tendencies that meta-historians have been encouraged to construct their systems. But in the last resort, trends produced in this way are always liable to individual divergences, and more frequently than the statisticians care to admit their predictions are falsified by changes in individual behaviour which they had no cause to expect. Recognition of this element of human quirkiness, of the irrepressibility of the human spirit, of the infinite diversity of personalities – in a word, of individuality – is thus the first and greatest lesson which can be learnt from a study of history.

An understanding of human individuality leads directly to another significant lesson of history – the perception that individual actions can be both benign and malevolent. Historians have frequently been bemused by hero-figures whom they have represented as paragons of virtue and talent against the lesser beings who have either followed the heroes or come into conflict with them. It cannot be denied that some men and women possess greater virtues and talents than others: such is the nature of individuality. But such hero-worship is unbecoming in an historian who is exceptionally well placed to perceive that heroes have blemishes and that their adversaries frequently have an understandable point of view. Man, outstandingly amongst the animal species, possesses the genius of individuality, but it is a flawed genius, enmeshed in conflicts of motive and tensions between self-interest and the aspirations to express a regard for others. Human nature, in short, is a most complex phenomenon, so that no one person can ever embody all the virtues or be without some of the blemishes. History, in its continuing record of human brilliance and human folly, provides an extraordinarily rich experience of this amalgam representing the diversity and ambiguity of human nature. It provides, that is to say, the means of appreciating the qualities of human beings and of sympathising with them in their complexities.

One of the most perplexing features of human nature is the problem of relating motives to actual achievement. The failure of people to fulfil their intentions, and their achievement of objectives which bear little relationship to their original aspirations, is a recurrent theme of all human history. This experience may be expressed in terms of good intentions leading to bad results, but to speak of 'good' and 'bad' in terms of human conduct is to introduce an element of ethical judgement into the discussion of human nature which is open to the charge of subjective moralising by the observer. Nevertheless, human beings have persistently used these ethical categories in determining their own action and in judging the actions of others, and the regularity with which good intentions have deteriorated into bad conduct has induced many ethical commentators to stress the quality of human fallibility and corruptibility by using a further ethical category, that of 'original sin' or a more secularised counterpart. The importance of this category is that it recognises one of the most profound aspects of human personality, namely, the tendency to qualify all aspirations, however lofty, by a reference to self-interest which invariably modifies the achievement of individuals in ways which alter the original goals. The tendency of power to corrupt, for instance, has become one of the clichés of historical scholarship, and in so far as it recognises the liability of individuals to be distracted from benevolent intentions by the pursuit of lesser motives, it spotlights one of the most momentous qualities of human nature.

By supplying abundant evidence of this 'gravitational bias' of human corruptibility, history thus teaches one of its most useful lessons. It is a lesson, however, which historians are not always anxious to learn or to impart. Belief in human 'perfectibility' has been persistent in Industrial Civilisation, and historians have not been unaffected by it. The holders of radical reformist political views are particularly prone to the conviction that men only behave badly because of some undesirable cultural influence – be it capitalism, the possession of private property, a defective educational system, or some other social 'abuse' – so that the removal of this influence will ensure good behaviour in the future. Apart from the unreality of believing that social conditions can be changed so easily, the fact is that there is no historical evidence whatsoever for the assumption that human nature can be significantly 'improved' in this way. On the contrary, there is abundant evidence that people who have grown up with near-ideal conditions tend to behave in exactly the same selfish and ambivalent way in which most people have always acted. Indeed, there is some evidence to suggest that 'camaraderie' and other qualities of 'good' social behaviour increase under pressure of what would normally be considered unfavourable conditions, to be dissipated once more when conditions improve. The much-lamented 'Dunkirk spirit' which flourished in Britain in circumstances of acute crisis during World War II is an excellent example of this tendency, but its disappearance in the post-war resumption of normality serves to emphasise the point of human unperfectibility. Human beings are capable of remarkable acts of self-sacrificial devotion, but the existence of self-interest and the actions which stem from it is, quite literally, a fact of life, and to deny it in any interpretation of the past or policy for the future is to deny the lessons of history.

Preferable Societies

If the experience of human nature made possible by a study of the past can be considered as the source of general lessons of history, the study of our own civilisation and its roots can provide more particular lessons, related to the social characteristics of human beings and their preferences for certain forms of social organisation. In the first place, a study of history supplies overwhelming demonstrations of the gregariousness of human beings: man is truly a social animal, depending on other human beings for the possibility of developing his capacities of creativity, and unable to survive for long in complete isolation from them. Thomas Hobbes observed that life in a hypothetical condition of individual isolation would be 'nasty, brutish, and short', and even though Daniel Defoe and others speculated about the survival of rational men in such isolation, the 'Robinson Crusoe' situation was regarded as an exercise in human ingenuity and resilience rather than an ideal society. The long period of maturation required by children in the human species determines a measure of stable social organisation, so that inter-dependence becomes a fact of human life from its outset.

This inescapable sociability of our species is worth emphasising because it serves to put us on our guard against various fashionable but specious arguments proposing the abolition of the family or the state. True, there is nothing sacrosanct about the way in which the family is organised in twentieth-century Industrial Civilisation, and it is certainly subject to many pressures to change, but the intrinsic biological and psychological need for some sort of family group providing support and stability for the young is not removed by any such conditions. Similarly, the arguments about the faults of particular states have been abundant in most periods of history in which political speculation has flourished, but they do not lead to the conclusion that the state is dispensable, and can therefore be expected to 'wither away'. Regarded as that society which ensures the integrity of a given group, both by maintaining good order within and defending it against attack from outside, the state is not dispensable. It is the most essential of all forms of human social organisation, for the simple reason that without a sound state all other forms of social relationship will disintegrate. History provides many lessons in the sort of destructive anarchy which follows the collapse of states, and conversely it offers little encouragement to those theoretical idealists who see in the disappearance of the state the way to liberty and human fulfilment. It is not necessary to say that such a consummation is impossible. It is enough to observe that the whole rich treasure house of human experience available to us through the study of history gives no ground for supposing that men and women can survive without a state for more than a few weeks.

Although the state is thus inescapable, the forms it may take are very varied, and we have observed the nature of the main varieties at an earlier point in this essay. As one of the particular lessons available from history, however, it is desirable to ask what evidence we can muster about the more preferable varieties of state. What can we learn from the past about the sort of state which we should aim at achieving in Industrial Civilisation? To a large extent, our choice is bound to be conditioned by the assumptions with which we approach the question. So let us grasp firmly the nettle of ethical judgements and declare that, on the strength of what we know about human nature, we would prefer those states which maximise the human capacities for creativity and self-expression, and that we would resist those states which constrain these faculties. The fact that many states, both in history and in the present, do constrain human self-expression beyond the minimum necessary to maintain social order is so obvious that it does not require illustration. Every despotism has attempted to do this in the interests of the despot, but in a more sophisticated way it can be attempted by other régimes in the interests of greater efficiency, the elimination of waste, the attainment of uniform standards of life, and other objectives which may be in themselves worthy and even desirable. But whatever their merits, it cannot be maintained that such régimes are conducive to the expression of individuality and human creativity.

The only societies in history which have positively welcomed these qualities of the human spirit have been the 'open societies' – those which have stressed the importance of individual involvement in decision-making and government, and which have devised institutions that have made such participation possible in the organisation of the state. These societies, and they are a minority in the millennia of historical civilisations, are those which have adopted democratic forms of government, beginning with Athens and some of the other Greek city-states and flowering briefly in some of the Italian city-states of the fourteenth and fifteenth centuries, and more emphatically in some of the nation-states of Industrial Civilisation in the nineteenth and twentieth centuries. It is not being suggested that the human spirit *only* expresses itself in such open societies. The Roman Empire was never able to subdue the Hellenic ferment of free enquiry. The princes who rose to power in the Italian city-states of the 'Quattrocento' found it advantageous for a time to patronise the Renaissance individualism of artists and scholars. And even the most oppressive despotisms of our own century have failed to stamp out resistance movements and dissidents. But if individuality and human self-expression are regarded as good things, requiring no further justification other than their capacity to allow men and women to fulfil their talents, then the weight of historical evidence points to the conclusion that democratic forms of government are preferable to all alternatives.

It has been argued earlier that democracy is a comparatively sophisticated form of government, because in stressing the importance of individual participation it implies a level of education and self-confidence which must be cultivated over a considerable period if the desirable measure of participation is to be achieved. This, again, is a lesson of history, as recent history has witnessed the collapse of many new democracies established with much good will in Africa and Asia, largely because they lacked the essential foundations of a sound educational system and a network of voluntary societies in which people could acquire the techniques of individual participation through discussion and committee work. The collapse of these democracies, to be replaced by military juntas and individual despots, may well have been regarded as inevitable in these circumstances, and it may be contended that the existing régimes maintain levels of organisational efficiency and social stability that would not have been within the competence of the democratic states which they replaced. No such judgement, however, affects in any way the conviction that, if individual human expression is good, then a democratic form of government is the best way of achieving it. Recent experience serves only to show the difficulties which are encountered on the road to this particular form of the 'good society'.

Keeping the Peace

In seeking to derive from history guidance about the sort of state at which we should aim in Industrial Civilisation, there is another component to consider – that of size. Growth has been such a general characteristic of our civilisation over the last thousand years, that we have become accustomed to all our units of reference, be they cities, industrial enterprises, or states, becoming larger and larger. Thus, the small feudal states of Western Europe combined into larger dynastic groupings and from these emerged the modern nation states. The discovery of vast new continents beyond Europe led to the expansion of these European nation states from the fifteenth to the nineteenth centuries, and the rivalry engendered by this expansive movement helped to inflame spirits of ardent nationalism which confirmed the territorial integrity of the parent states in Europe.

The present century, as we have seen, has experienced dramatic changes in this disposition of world power. The European nation-states have been eclipsed by the super-states of the United States, the Soviet Union, and China. The states of the 'Third World' have risen to a strident but influential role in world politics. And some of the ancient rivals of European power politics have begun to pool their economic resources in order to find collective solutions to the social and political problems which perplex them. However, the inviolability of the sovereignty of the nation-state, elevated to a political dogma in the nineteenth century, has still not been seriously challenged, despite the existence of the United Nations Organisation since World War II. The time has surely come to question this dogma, because the survival of a multitude of nation states, each maintaining its sovereign right to make war on any other state, is the most serious danger to the stability of the modern world, posing a perpetual threat of triggering off the nuclear holocaust to avoid which should be the primary object of political strategy.

We have no way of foretelling in detail the effects of an all-out nuclear war, and it would be worse than foolhardy to seek experimental demonstration of these effects. There can be no doubt, however, that they would be very serious, involving the death of millions of people, the destruction of cities, and possibly the permanent pollution of the atmosphere so that advanced life would not survive or would undergo unpredictable mutations. Some military experts argue that the species has survived mass slaughter and destruction in the past, and calculate that it is likely to do so in the future. The human species has, indeed, been remarkably resilient to catastrophe and unavoidable changes in the environment, and it is conceivable that it could adjust itself to living in a world contaminated by radioactive fall-out. But however tenaciously mankind contrived to survive a disaster of this magnitude, it would almost certainly bring about a reversal to a primitive, self-supporting, tribal sort of society. Almost as terrible would be the unavoidable conclusion of such a collapse, that mankind is not capable of the measure of self-discipline necessary to ensure the survival of an advanced social organisation. If man cannot escape from the dilemma of self-destruction on this occasion, there is no reason to believe that he will perform any better in the future. The bleak prospect of civilisation and the human species would thus become one of successive phases of disaster and recovery until such time as a war occurred of such overwhelming devastation that man would finally destroy himself.

The prospect of another world war is so dreadful that all the resources of Industrial Civilisation should be applied to its prevention. The popular argument, current in the press and parliaments of the western democracies, that the nation-states of the world can delay war indefinitely by a process of mutual deterrence, is a delusion. As long as the nations are preparing for nuclear war, as they are at present, nuclear war is possible, and the possibility tends to increase with the passage of time because people become familiar with the expectation and resigned to its consequences. Recognising the historical cycle whereby there has been a major war in every generation since the rise of the nation-state to political power in Europe, this possibility is converted into a probability and even into a certainty, although the determinist implication of such a forecast depends upon the assumption that there is no change in the conditions of national sovereignty on which it is based. The only course of action which can prevent war is that of cutting through national animosities by the creation of a viable world government. Even a world government will give no final guarantee of peace, for 'civil' wars would still be possible within the world-state, and as long as man possesses the technological competence for self-destruction, the threat that it may some day be used will hang over his head like the legendary sword of Damocles. But in so far as man can erect institutional bulwarks against the danger of nuclear war, the sacrifice of national sovereignty in a federated world-state is an essential step.

Our survey of the historical developments of the nation-states of Europe has recognised that there are real differences of race, language, and tradition between them. These difficulties cannot be dismissed either by ignoring them or by an ideological slanging match. They require a prolonged effort of imaginative understanding on the part of every nation towards every other nation. Given such a quality in our international relationships, and given also patient diplomacy and a reasonable amount of good luck, the present unstable equilibrium between the nation-states of the world may be maintained for a further five, ten, or even twenty years. But ultimately the only hope of lasting peace is to use such a breathing space in order to escape from the antagonisms in which nation-states are placed by their insistence on complete autonomy and sovereignty. The creation of a world-state fulfils the basic requirement of this liberation, because it removes from nation-states the sovereign right of each to make war on the others as it chooses.

Although the concept of a world-state is regarded as unrealistic and impractical in much contemporary political debate, there is at least one eloquent historical precedent which proves that it is both realistic and practical. This is the success of the United States of America in fusing a number of distinct states with different and even conflicting interests within the structure of a single federal government. The initial constitution was adopted by the thirteen states which threw off British rule in 1776, and it has proved sufficiently flexible to assimilate additional states at intervals ever since, and to absorb a vast immigrant population which has caused the United States to be described as the 'melting pot' of nationalities. Member states have retained a significant identity with distinct powers, but this has not prevented the growth of a strong federal authority capable of wielding decisive influence in international affairs. Admittedly, the American Civil War demonstrated the fact that even a flexible federal constitution does not prevent the possibility of bitter fratricidal conflict. But the American experience provides a valuable example, in microcosm, of how a world-state could work. It shows that, contrary to a widely held belief, mere size is not an insuperable problem for a world government, because the powers of any number of subsidiary units can be ensured whatever the size of the federal whole.

The analogy is an instructive one, and should serve to show that *structural* arguments against a world government are without foundation. In accepting the principle of federation, existing nation-states could surrender immediately those aspects of sovereign power which assert their autonomy in relations with other nation-states, and yet continue with their own internal self-government unchanged. Of course it would be important to harmonise juridical and administrative practices between members of the international federation, but this could be a gradual process and there would be no need to insist on the uniformity of internal governments as a condition of membership. Moreover, such an international federation could begin as soon as any two states get together to establish it, welcoming such other states as can be persuaded to join in the future. Far from being difficult to achieve, the structural aspects of world government are thus eminently practical. The objections to it spring almost entirely from the strong sense of nationalism which has become such a powerful tradition in Industrial Civilisation. Even here, however, there is no necessary conflict. To many of its most able protagonists, nationalism has been a noble ideal leading to internationalism, and there is no reason why national characteristics or other regional loyalties should be lost under a world government, save that, as with the differences between Lancashire and Yorkshire, it should no longer seem desirable to go to war in order to defend them.

In one sense, the experience of recent history has not favoured the cause of world government, because the record of international bodies such as the League of Nations and the United Nations Organisation has failed to sustain the idealistic hopes of their founders. Those organisations appear repeatedly to have failed or been ineffective when confronted by a crisis between member states.

The fact is, however, that they have failed precisely because they have lacked the powers of a world government, and yet the notion of world government has suffered through association with their failures. This is not to criticise the UN in any way: quite the contrary, the organisation performs prodigies of international administration, providing highly beneficial services to the nations of the world, in the face of tremendous obstacles. In a world lacking genuine agents of international government, the UN is the closest approximation and deserves all the support it can get. But the reality of the situation should not be ignored, and in order to achieve genuine world government it will be necessary either radically to alter the present constitution of the UN, vesting in its Security Council and officers powers over member states which they do not at present possess, or to set up a world federation of nation-states on a fresh basis. Of the two courses of action, the second is the simpler, because any two nations can come together to frame an open-ended constitution creating a federal body to which they and future members will surrender certain of their sovereign powers. An initiative by a number of leading states in taking these preliminary steps towards the creation of a world government could transform the whole context of international relationships. It would show a way of moving from the image of the jungle suggested by the spectacle of nation-states asserting their strength through a free-for-all display of military might, to an era of creative co-operation by states united in their allegiance to a single terrestrial authority.

The lessons of history are many and varied. In this chapter, however, we have been concerned only to establish the principle that history can provide useful guidance in present actions and future policy, and to suggest some of the ways in which this guidance can be abstracted from the experience of our civilisation and its predecessors. We have been concerned especially with the general insight which a study of history can give into the complexity of human nature, hoping thereby to emphasise the importance which individuality deserves to receive. More particularly, we have tried to show how historical experience suggests that there are good reasons for taking democratic forms of government seriously as those which are most appropriate to a society stressing human individuality and creativity; and that there are equally pressing reasons for pursuing policies which will lead towards the establishment of a genuine world government. Clearly, as was observed at the outset of this discussion, the nature of the lessons which are derived from history will be determined largely by the assumptions with which the resources of history are approached, and the lessons outlined here are no exception. But the assumptions are so basic to our civilisation – a belief in human nature, good government, and in the desirability of avoiding war – that the historical evidence which can be marshalled in their elucidation cannot be regarded as irrelevant to the contemporary problem of the world. History, in the last resort, cannot solve our problems: only we can do that. What it can do is to illuminate these problems with an intensity which no other discipline can provide, equipping the citizens of today with a temporal dimension which can help them to understand their problems and thus to work out better solutions to them.

10. The Prospects of Industrial Civilisation

History is, in part, a search for precedents – an interpretation of the past designed to indicate similarities and congruities in order to suggest lessons which can be applied to the present and the future so that our performance may be improved. It has been with this purpose that we have explored some of the most important themes in the development of modern Industrial Civilisation. The description of the exercise as an 'exploration' is appropriate because the treatment of many large subjects has undoubtedly been perfunctory. Some, indeed, have been dealt with in only a few words, and even with those chosen for examination in more detail little more than a preliminary survey has been possible. Nevertheless, even this cavalier treatment has sufficed to show the essential unity of our civilisation, and the shape of the problems which confront it and which require solutions in this generation. The argument of the preceding pages, in short, has been that Industrial Civilisation has arrived at a point of momentous significance in its development. In an over-worked but realistic metaphor, it is at a cross-roads, where a collective decision has to be made between alternative courses of action. In the generation of those of us who are alive now, decisions will be made, either explicitly or by default, which will affect the character of our civilisation, and even its survival. If it is to have a worth-while future, everything will depend on the wisdom and timeliness of our collective action in the last quarter of the twentieth century. The destiny of the species is in our hands. Never in human history has so much depended upon the decisions of a single generation of men and women.

With this awesome responsibility in mind, an attempt is made in this concluding chapter to make some tentative extrapolations or projections on the basis of the historical interpretation which has been expounded in the previous chapters. We will consider, first, the nature of the problems confronting contemporary society, and particularly those problems concerned with the control of growth. Then we will cast our projections further into the future, to examine the long-term possibilities of various alternative developments, and the sort of challenges with which they will present mankind.

The Midas Touch

King Midas, according to the fable, was so devoted to gold that he made a wish that everything he touched would change into the precious metal. The wish was duly granted, but the king's initial delight, when all the chairs and tables within his reach were converted into solid gold, was changed into horror when the food he tried to eat and the favourite princess whom he kissed underwent a similar transformation. Overcome by remorse, he begged that his wish might be rescinded.

Industrial Civilisation owes its unique dynamic quality to its discovery of the Midas-touch: to the ability to produce a continuing and accumulating volume of material wealth. The discovery was made and refined in Western Civilisation between AD 1000 and 1750, and was then passed on through the medium of industrialisation to the world civilisation which succeeded it and which is now enjoying the results of a thousand years of expanding wealth-creation. Unfortunately, as with the experience of King Midas, the process has not worked out quite as its participants hoped, and there has been much anxiety about some of its harmful consequences, such as the population explosion which threatens to consume all the benefits of greater material wealth. But unlike the king in the parable, it is useless to think of our civilisation abandoning the gift of continuing wealth-creation. The world population which has expanded in response to new wealth can now only be sustained by the process of industrialisation, so that to revert to a simpler form of society would involve colossal social disruption. For better or for worse, Industrial Civilisation has become dependent upon the Midas-touch. The gift which has been the cause of many of its problems must now be used to solve these problems.

We have already seen how the mainspring of Western growth – the Midas-touch – was a combination of possibilities for expansion with a powerful motivation to take advantage of these possibilities. The prospect of almost limitless expansion opened up for Western

Civilisation with the fifteenth-century voyages of discovery and continued into the twentieth century with the relentless pursuit of settlement and increasing productivity along those 'frontiers' where the expansive culture of industrialisation pressed upon the comparatively empty and underdeveloped parts of the world. The motivation to take advantage of this expansion was provided partly by national rivalries, but more significantly by a particular temper of mind to which we have applied the term 'puritanism'. Taking it out of its strictly religious context, we have interpreted puritanism as the psychological drive for self-justification, sustained by a rigorous will to discipline immediate needs and appetites in the interest of long-term benefits. Such a spirit animated the men who fashioned the techniques of wealth-creation, often with considerable sacrifice and ruthlessness. Their discipline, however harsh on both themselves and others, secured the surplus needed for re-investment to ensure that the European financial system, the apparatus of capitalism, and the ability to promote technological innovations, operated harmoniously together to drive the intricate engine of wealth-creation. Once established, the engine acquired sufficient momentum to ride out local collapses and failures of motivation. It produced the material substance to support an upward surge of the world population at a standard of living which, while not noticeably improving for the mass of people, enabled a significant minority to enjoy a better quality of life. This, as we have previously argued, has been an astonishing achievement for Industrial Civilisation and has demonstrated its dynamic ability to create the essential components of human wealth on a scale which would have been unimaginable only a few generations ago.

However, the Midas-touch has been a mixed blessing. Not only have the number of mouths to be fed threatened constantly to outdistance the capacity of an expanding industrial economy to feed them, but the essential restraints on present consumption in order to maintain the surplus for re-investment in the wealth-creating engine have become increasingly onerous to people looking for satisfaction in the short term rather than in the prospect of 'pie in the sky when they die'. Simultaneously, the engine of wealth-creation is showing alarming signs of failure, and in precisely those qualities which were essential to its initial success: the possibilities of expansion, whether economically or demographically, seem to be declining rapidly as the development 'frontiers' of the world have nearly all been rolled back;

and the stimulus of a powerful motivation, deriving from national rivalries or from a high level of individual commitments and self-discipline, have become discernibly weaker since the end of World War II. Of course, new international rivalries have replaced those which were exhausted by the Thirty-One Years War of the twentieth century, but the main problem in these relationships, as was discussed in the last chapter, is that of achieving at least a stalemate situation and more hopefully a genuine movement towards world government. The factor of national rivalry is thus highly ambiguous: it has certainly promoted wealth-creation by economic growth in the past, but it has also caused the loss of wealth through armed conflict on a gargantuan scale, and there can be little doubt that its influence in a world such as ours, poised delicately on the edge of a nuclear holocaust, is likely to be more harmful than beneficial.

Thus we find ourselves in a situation where our techniques for wealth-creation have been so extraordinarily successful that they have triggered off a world population explosion, while they appear to be losing some of their powers to cope with the variegated problems caused by this increased fecundity of the human species. Perhaps we are in danger of losing the Midas-touch, at a moment when we most urgently require it. Prognosticators are not lacking in the modern world to tell us that we are heading for catastrophe. There was a lively but inconclusive controversy in the early 1970s, generated by increasing ecological anxiety and particularly by the energy crisis which loomed suddenly as a result of war in the Middle East, about the desirability of continuing growth. One group of experts, represented by the 'Club of Rome', made sophisticated computer projections of the growth trends in Industrial Civilisation and concluded that on virtually every count disaster was imminent if these trends continued. Other experts countered this doom-laden forecast by stressing the historical capacity of the leading growth factors to respond to social needs and market pressures, so that what was needed was not so much a cessation of growth as its re-distribution.[1] The inconclusive nature of the debate reflects differences of emphasis amongst the contestants. The pessimists were most alarmed by the population explosion and the related problems of food production, whereas the optimists tended to stress the ingenuity of science and technology in finding alternative sources of energy and substitutes for other resources which are threatened with rapid depletion. Also, it was possible to fault the methods by which the pessimistic computer projections had been made, and thus to confuse what had seemed a fairly simple issue of arriving at Doomsday. If nothing else, the controversy demonstrated the complexity of the problems and the manifold interconnections between their various components.

The debate, however, is too important to be shrugged off on the grounds that, as even the experts are divided on the subject, it must be beyond the competence of ordinary citizens to come to a judgement about it. At the very least we should respond to the warning that growth itself cannot be regarded as necessarily beneficial, in the way that has been assumed for much of the last generation by international authorities, national governments, and municipal planners. It is indeed apparent that some aspects of the near-exponential growth of the last 200 years present most formidable difficulties. Outstandingly, this is the case with population growth, for unless this can be brought under control all other forms of growth will be consumed in coping with it. In this case, growth is inimical to social progress, and will hinder the achievement of any goal by our society other than a mere increase in numbers.

Once it is recognised that not all forms of growth can coexist, it becomes necessary not to condemn them all but to decide which should be encouraged and which discouraged. This can only be done by establishing a clear definition of the objectives or goals of our society. If we get no further than welcoming all increases in production as indices of progress, our 'goals' are likely to be nothing more than milestones on the road to oblivion. However difficult and value-ridden a more discriminating assessment of objectives may be, it will be preferable to such empirical pragmatism. As an interim objective, Industrial Civilisation could usefully adopt a model of stable equilibrium. This would involve, first, the urgent and daunting task of achieving world demographic stability within the next century. It would involve, also, a diligent application to the problems raised by the depletion of irreplaceable mineral resources, and to the need for ecological balance and environmental conservation on a global scale. And it would involve, thirdly, a sustained political programme aimed at redistributing the fruits of economic growth so that all members of the world community came to share in a rising standard of living. Within the context of a world government on the lines already discussed, such a programme would have a high priority. World government, it should be emphasised, would be an integral feature of any viable model of stable equilibrium, being the only way of providing the necessary institutional apparatus of world demographic and ecological controls, and means for the redistribution of wealth to achieve all-round increases in standards of living.

Stable equilibrium is thus a worthy objective for Industrial Civilisation in the twentieth century, because it adopts a discriminating attitude towards economic growth, on a basis of social justice which would be widely acknowledged. It presents a realisable goal in the shape of a world community using its creative powers to achieve a good society for all its members. It remains, nevertheless, an interim goal, because there are longer-term objectives which must be defined. However desirable as a breathing space, allowing mankind to put its metaphorical house, spaceship Earth, in order, it may be argued that stability is not a natural condition for Industrial Civilisation, and that historical experience indicates a need for continuing expansion and for a powerful sense of human motivation. The Midas-touch, in short, has set us on a pattern of social evolution from which we can only depart by collapse or self-destruction. Even the achievement of stable equilibrium by the end of the twentieth century can only be a springboard from which mankind must tackle larger problems and undertake longer-term missions.[2]

Alternative Futures

When Plato wrote *The Republic*, he took as his central theme in describing the desiderata and institutions of his ideal society the idea of justice. Having, through the mouth of Socrates, abolished other conceptions of justice, Plato presented his own version as a condition of society in which every person occupies the position appropriate to him. Thus, the man trained to be the philosopher-king is leader, the men best able to fight comprise the army, the trained craftsmen practise their skills, and so on. Admittedly, this is too élitist a conception of justice to be popular in contemporary society, and it does not seem to have had much following in Plato's own time. But it provides a useful starting-point for a consideration of possible future societies because it represents a particularly impressive intellectual attempt to present an ideal society. Since Plato, many thinkers have offered alternative models of ideal societies. Thomas More, for instance, invented the term 'Utopia' to describe his own vision, and thereby provided a label for this whole category of imaginative literature. Not many of these are readable or even interesting, although it should be said that More's own account is one which is still fascinating, with its vigorous polemic against social conditions in early Tudor England and its colourful description of the organisation of Utopia.[3] Some of them, like Samuel Butler's *Erewhon*, have a highly ironical and satirical content, while others again, like Huxley's *Brave New World* and Orwell's *1984*, portray similar models of possible futures as warnings rather than as objects for emulation.

The range of blue-prints for alternative futures available in the utopian (and distopian) literature is thus very wide, so that it could be a long process securing any general agreement about which design should be adopted at any particular time and place. It is, however, of crucial importance to any strategy for survival, even in the short-term, to have some basic understanding of what constitutes the good society which that strategy is seeking to achieve or to preserve. The aspects considered in our discussion so far – keeping the peace through world government, controlling the population explosion, and achieving a measure of ecological balance – are objectives which can be planned for by a series of pragmatic decisions once the target has been determined. But in themselves, they may not secure anything worth securing. In recent world history, Nazi Germany is a salutary example of a society which sought to establish world peace by imposing the Thousand Year Reich on the pattern of previous conquering empires, and the Nazis also devised an efficient policy for disposing of unwanted population. This, however, was the prescription for government by criminal thugs, and was morally indefensible. What was lacking was a commonly accepted goal of a desirable society. That is why agreement about goals is necessary if any strategy for survival is to be successful in the modern world.

Limited agreement about desirable goals should be obtainable on the basis of an historical understanding of the development of Industrial Civilisation. In particular, it should be possible to agree that the ideal society must be democratic, if only for the reason that democracy offers most people the opportunity for responsibility and self-expression. There is abundant historical evidence to show that, whatever criticisms may be levelled against it, democracy offers more scope for the fulfilment of individuality than rival forms of collective organisation. The other reasons for preferring democracy to alternative forms of government are also powerful: the rule of law is better than the rule of the autocrat (except possibly for the autocrat); the possibility of participation in the processes of decision-making helps the individual to a mature appreciation of his rights and duties as a citizen; the need for effective voluntary societies and for a widely based educational system can only be satisfied under a democratic régime; and the scope for individual creativity is significantly greater in a democracy than under any other form of government. These preferences, of course, reflect value judgements, but they are judgements formed by reflecting on the historical experience of Industrial Civilisation and deciding, on balance, which forms of society and which derivative institutions are most likely to promote the vitality and survival of our society. As these are the objects of our concern, it should be clear that there are impressive reasons for concluding that the best possible organisation to ensure the endurance of Industrial Civilisation is a democratic society. If our strategy for survival is to succeed, therefore, it is necessary that our struggle to establish world peace and to achieve a stable equilibrium in demographic and ecological pressures should be contained within a democratically conceived framework of the rule of law and responsible participation. Otherwise we may struggle to survive only to find that we have preserved an empty shell and that, deprived of its noblest and most creative values, our civilisation will have entered another Dark Age.

However reasonable an objective of social policy may seem when presented in a rational discussion, it cannot be assumed that it will automatically be adopted even by those who consider it. The goal of a democratic society in a posture of stable equilibrium has to compete with other programmes possessing powerful motivations derived from such sources as religious belief, political nationalism, and a short-term appraisal of immediate self-interest. It is true that there is an important component of self-interest in any strategy for survival, and the objective of democratic stable equilibrium is no exception in this respect. But to a considerable extent the stress is on deferred or long-term self-interest, so that it can easily come into conflict with the promise of immediate rewards, however temporary their effect. As for the opposition posed by alternative religions or political beliefs, it is important that the pursuit of democratic stable equilibrium should be sustained by corresponding beliefs and motivations which are able to respond to the challenge. It is necessary to present the social goals which are rationally desirable with the support of convictions based on religious belief and political commitment. Only in this way can the strength of a rational argument be converted into the enthusiasm of a mass movement capable of enduring indefinitely.

In our examination of the development of Industrial Civilisation and the Western Civilisation from which it grew we have had to observe on several occasions the crucial role of religion in formulating objectives and providing the motivation necessary to pursue these objectives. In particular, we emphasised the significance of those religious groups to which, for want of a better term, we gave the name 'puritanism', in supplying the dedication and moral earnestness without which the more painful aspects of industrialisation could not have been achieved. Puritan motivation was, without any doubt, religious in a conventional sense: that is to say, it was inspired by a belief in a supernatural god and a life after death in which rewards earned during a man's earthly pilgrimage would be achieved. The story of Bunyan's Christian has been an eloquent illustration of this puritan conception of the pilgrim's progress. Such puritan belief has been undermined by the advance of secularisation. The question must be asked, therefore, whether or not any kind of belief requiring dedication, self-discipline, and a readiness to sacrifice immediate interests is attainable in the secular post-Christian society of modern Industrial Civilisation?

Secularisation is the secular habit of thought, arising out of science and industrialisation. It asserts the autonomy of the various fields of human endeavour against any attempt to impose a supra-rational authority, and it assumes that life can be explained in rational and scientific terms, denying the validity of any resort to magic or supernaturalism. Secularisation is thus opposed to the intellectual dominance of any particular religion, but it is not necessarily hostile to religion as an integrating philosophy of life, particularly when that philosophy integrates the main assumptions of secularisation. Provided that religion is not equated with supernaturalism, there is no necessary opposition between it and secularisation. Science may not possess the means of answering all the ultimate questions about the nature of time and the purpose of life with which religion has been traditionally concerned. But science has become the dominant element in modern culture, and as in science whatever is, is natural, and is the legitimate subject of scientific investigation, it may be taken as axiomatic that any successful religion of the future will have no room for magic or the supernatural. If this insistence on naturalism and rationality can be accepted, however, there would seem to be no insuperable obstacle to the development of a thoroughly secular religion.[4]

It follows from this brief analysis that the idea of a sort of secular puritanism should not be ruled out as being necessarily a contradiction in terms. If the main function of religion is seen as being that of providing answers to the ultimate questions of life and death, then the role of religion has still to be performed, even in a secular society, if people are to behave meaningfully and creatively. When the traditional institutions of religion fail to do this adequately – as they have failed to do for most of the last 100 years – other ideas are available to act as secular substitutes. We have seen in the historical record of our civilisation how effectively concepts such as nationalism and progress have fulfilled this pressing human desire for purpose, meaning, and motivation. There is thus no lack of secular religions at the disposal of modern man. What is important is to establish the principles of a good society in such a way that it is possible to reconcile the dedicated motivation of puritanism with the objectives of secularised aspirations.

The key to such a reconciliation is the idea of brotherhood. We have previously had cause to observe that kinship alone does not solve all problems of personal relationships. The story of Cain and Abel, and the experience of every 'civil' war in history, make this reservation forcefully. But the success of the policies which we have been outlining in this chapter, charting a course amongst alternative futures towards a truly desirable sort of society – is in the last resort utterly dependent upon the creation of a sense of emotional kinship, a brotherhood of mankind. Only such a sense of belonging together can give the human species any hope of surviving in the face of the formidable problems and daunting tasks that confront it at the end of the twentieth century. The ethic of brotherhood is at least as old as the major religions, in all of which it appears. But it has hitherto been generally limited to their own fellow-believers: the faithful brethren have been defined in contrast with the barbarians, the infidels, and the heretics.

The ideal of Fraternity blossomed briefly in the wake of the European revolutionary movement and romantic fervour of the beginning of the nineteenth century. Schiller expressed this sentiment in the verse put to inspired music by Beethoven: 'Alle Menschen werden Brüder'. But if, indeed, all men were to be brothers, it was essential that they should abandon divisive notions like militant nationalism and racialism, and in the context of that epoch of competitive expansion and bitter national rivalries this was not possible. So the idea of brotherhood was diluted and then ignored in the destructive pursuit of short-term national interest. Now, at a time when alternative religions have faltered or proved themselves inadequate to cope with the problems of contemporary Industrial Civilisation in sustaining human dignity and purposeful motivation, there is a greater need than ever before for a strongly-held ethic of world brotherhood. It provides a plausible answer both to the ultimate religious questions and to the problems of our time. It provides a goal to aim at and a cause to fight for. It offers what may well be, without dramatic exaggeration, the last chance of mankind to adopt a mission which will enable him to survive the consequences of his own brilliant but wayward creativity.

Perspectives of Time

In a recent popular book, Alvin Toffler has drawn attention to the consequences of 'Future Shock', by which he means the stress, both physical and psychological, to which people are subjected today by the accelerating tempo of social change.[5] The study is historically superficial, but in so far as it emphasises the drastic changes which have taken place in the life-styles of citizens of Industrial Civilisation in the twentieth century, it serves to illustrate one of the most significant features of our own historical analysis – the unique quality of modern industrial society, without any close precedent in historical experience. This element of novelty makes the task of projecting historical trends forward into the future particularly difficult and speculative. But it also makes the task all the more important, in order to establish some sort of marker-posts or goals which will give us a sense of direction in coping with unprecedented situations. We have already made considerable progress, in this chapter, in outlining a sketch-map of possible and desirable futures. Now we must attempt one more step, and enquire what guidance our historical experience can provide in taking some long-term projections regarding the future prospects of Industrial Civilisation and whatever comes after it.

To begin with, an understanding of historical processes can give an illuminating perspective from which to scan the future. The most profound cultural shock, amounting virtually to a spiritual trauma, in the experience of man, has been the new view of the universe forced upon him by his own increasingly skilful scientific observations. The fact that we now take this trauma very much for granted does not lessen the significance of its impact on our minds. Only four centuries ago everybody except a handful of Copernican astronomers still regarded the Earth as the centre around which the rest of the universe revolved, and in the minds of most people this image of Earth's centrality merged into that of the mythological three-tier universe with the Earth placed securely between Heaven above and Hades below. With the Newtonian revolution in scientific thought these traditional images of man's central status in the universe began to fade, but they did not do so immediately or completely. For one thing, it remained possible, even with Newton's model of infinite space, to conceive of that space as occupied by a random and insignificant amount of matter with the sun at its centre, bearing on its planet Earth the only species made by God with the divine gift of intelligence. This essentially conservative view was confirmed by the conviction that the whole universe had been created at a point in time only shortly before recorded history began, a mere six or seven millennia ago. So long as this belief went unchallenged, the unique centrality of the human species remained axiomatic, and as even the great Newton had accepted this foreshortened time-scale without question it required considerable courage or foolhardiness to challenge it.

Yet challenged it was, in a variety of ways. The first way in which evidence began to accumulate of things being different from the traditional assumptions was through the patient exploration of Newtonian space by astronomers. It gradually became apparent, in the eighteenth and nineteenth centuries, that the size of the observable universe was a great deal larger than anybody had imagined. It was one thing to accept an abstract theoretical idea of infinite space, but to find that space filled with more and more stars as telescopes probed its depths was another matter. The picture began to emerge of the sun being a single star in a vast star-field, beyond which other equally gigantic clusters of stars or galaxies could be discerned. Compared with other stars it appeared that the sun was in no way a remarkable specimen, being of somewhat less than average size and brilliancy. In these circumstances, it was difficult to continue holding the traditional belief in human uniqueness.

Even more shattering, however, was the dawning of the realisation that the Earth was much older than the axiomatic seven millennia. Evidence from the study of geology provided the vital clues at the beginning of the nineteenth century, and Charles Darwin demonstrated that on the basis of the extended geological time-scale it was possible to explain the enormously complex processes of organic development and variation by natural selection, without recourse to the traditional assumption of special creation by divine fiat. The triumph of evolutionary interpretations in geology and the life sciences was accompanied by the increasing confidence of progressivistic interpretations of human history, and by the acceptance of a long ancestry for mankind in a way which linked him intimately with other species and interpreted him as merely the last link in a long evolutionary chain.[6]

Thus *homo sapiens* has with increasing knowledge lost his estimation of his own supremacy and uniqueness. Admittedly he has not as yet encountered (so far as he can tell at present) any other intelligent species which can conclusively deprive him of this unique status, and he has discovered no evidence to date for life at any other point in the universe, apart from the tantalising but inconclusive hints of the first experiments to search for the existence of life on Mars in 1976. So it remains a possibility that he is on his own, as an intelligent form of life, in this incredibly large, ancient, and puzzling universe. Statistically, however, the chances of man being unique are negligible, and the possibility that he is rather one of literally millions of such intelligent species in this galaxy alone has to be taken seriously. It is this imperative to take seriously his role in the expanded dimensions of space and time revealed by the persistence of his own enquiries that constitutes the ultimate destiny of mankind. It is his cosmic mission to explore the universe.

To put it baldly in this way is to raise a banner, not to prove an argument. The argument, indeed, is not open to proof in the sense that a discussion of historical or contemporary events might be. Only time – and a lot of time at that – can provide the conclusive sort of demonstration that may be acceptable as proof of the proposition. That is why commitment to it is primarily a matter of orientation and motivation – a result of the sort of secular religion which has been proposed. It depends, that is to say, more on the sort of society we wish to create than on the demonstrable facts of what has already been created. But there is sufficient evidence available already to show that such a commitment is far from being unrealistic, and that it offers mankind the long-term goal which he needs and which is better than any alternative aspiration. The evidence is worth summarising.

First, there are clear literary indications that mankind is beginning to take a really long-term view of his prospects in terms of alternative visions of the future. This is an encouraging development, because the customary attitude of the traditional religions and philosophies towards the future has been evasive. It is something 'stored up in Heaven' or 'in the Paradise to come', and when it has been discussed at all it has usually been on a foreshortened time-scale as if the Last Things were about to happen. Even Marxist dialectical materialism lacks precision in its definition of conditions in the Promised Land of the Proletarian Revolution. Thought about the future of our species could hardly begin to assume a systematic form until the intellectual acceptance of evolution and progress, and of man's isolation in an infinitely perplexing universe. The first genuine examples of the 'science fiction' genre were therefore the product of the late nineteenth-century intellectual revolution which made it possible to think in this way. Since then, the volume of imaginative writing in the science fiction category has risen both in output and width of market appeal, if not always in quality.

There can be little doubt that much science fiction of the 'bug-eyed monster' type is of a low literary standard, but there is also much that has demonstrated remarkably imaginative and accurate perceptions of likely lines of development. The significance of science fiction in this context is not so much its literary quality as its existence as a distinct type of intellectual exercise. In science fiction creative writers have been seeking for the first time to explore the frontiers of human possibilities and probabilities. With the aid of ingeniously constructed charts of possible heavens and hells these writers have been directing the thoughts of the last two generations towards the future of mankind. Some of their suggestions have already proved to be prophetic, while others have been overtaken by events and shown to be ludicrously inaccurate. In many respects concerning short-term projections, the best science fiction writers have tended to allow rather more time for their ideas to be worked out than has been necessary in real life. Taken collectively, this genre has added a new and still unfamiliar dimension to the human psyche – speculation about the future of man and the universe. It is a most significant portent of the imaginative capabilities unleashed by Industrial Civilisation that it has begun to make this intellectual exploration, and it is a clue, to say the least, of the awakening consciousness of a cosmic mission for mankind.[7]

The second category of evidence regarding the immediate relevance of long-term projections about the future of mankind is that of the dramatic developments of the space programmes launched by the United States and the Soviet Union in the late 1950s. The Russian success in putting the first 'sputnik' into orbit in 1957 was followed by a massive but ill-defined 'space race' with the two super-powers seeking primacy in achieving ever more remote and complex goals. The result has been a staggering efflorescence of space technology which has brought, within two decades, the mastery of orbital flight and the beginning of manned space laboratories; the exploration of the moon by photography, mechanised instrumentation, and by human beings; the beginning of surveys of Mercury, Venus, and Mars, including in the last two cases the landing of instruments on the surface; and the dispatch of further-ranging space probes, the first of which are now out beyond the planet Jupiter and will eventually escape completely from the gravitational field of the sun. These developments have been supported by equally remarkable progress in electronics, micro-miniaturisation, long-distance control techniques, radio-astronomy, and numerous other technologies. In a very substantial sense, the Space Age has been inaugurated in the last two decades. Only the fact that the excitement of rocket launches and space triumphs has become a regular source of news has caused us to take such achievements for granted and prevented us from making a full appraisal of their significance. The programme of space exploration is in danger of being a victim of its own success.

Of course, one sort of appraisal is to dismiss the whole space programme as a colossal waste of the world's resources, and such criticisms have been expressed in many parts of the world. Certainly, the cost of the programme has been immmense by current standards of international finance and it is arguable that the resources consumed by it could have been put to more immediately productive use in raising world living standards and achieving other eminently worth-while objectives such as the other short-term goals which we have already discussed. Unfortunately, it is not likely that resources saved by the early cancellation of the space programme would have been reallocated in this way. The world is still too divided into national compartments to make such a flow of resources possible, and there would have been no stimulus to national effort comparable to the 'space race' which might have promoted the transfer. What seems more likely is that the space programme absorbed resources which would otherwise have found their way into the supreme human idiocy of the international armaments race, and in so far as the space race is preferable to the armaments race the space programme deserves to be welcomed. Moreover, almost will-nilly, the space race has led to a greater mutual respect between the superpowers and to the start of a sharing in space expertise which, although small, is of momentous significance. It serves to make the point, indeed, that a high priority in promoting the space programme is that it provides a token of pacific intentions and helps to improve the atmosphere of international relations. Despite their expense, therefore, it is doubtful whether the space programmes of the superpowers have affected substantially the level of their assistance to deprived groups at home or in other nations, and it is certain that they have contributed to a more cordial understanding between nations. They have thus proved their value as an investment, and it must be hoped that the initiative of space exploration will not be relinquished now that it has been firmly seized. In terms of the total resources of the great powers, the financial investment in space in the immediate future will be quite modest. The cost of the privilege of living in the Space Age is thus remarkably light.

In addition to the increasing imaginative familiarity with the future prospects of mankind and the existence of impressive achievements from two decades of Space Age technology, there is a third category of evidence in support of a long-term commitment to a cosmic mission for mankind. It brings us back to the historical analysis of Industrial Civilisation with which we have been concerned in previous chapters. We emphasised there the important function performed by the possibility of expansion in the growth of our civilisation. From the medieval crusades, through the voyages of discovery to nineteenth-century imperialism and the rolling back of the internal 'frontiers' in the newly occupied continents (so far as Industrial Civilisation was concerned) of America, Africa, and Australia, the pioneering spirit has provided an outlet for land-hungry people, a stimulus to trade and transport, an incentive to banking facilities and technological innovation, and a pretext for colonial settlement and political appropriation. While it is not suggested that these have always been desirable qualities, there can be no doubt that they have been evidence of dynamic development and that they have served to relieve tensions such as over-population in the parent territories which, without the solution of expansion, would have created severe economic problems and might have caused stagnation or breakdown. There are many historical precedents for such a deterioration of economic conditions when the facility for expansion has been lost, and with the complete taming of the last empty spaces on the surface of the earth, the moment is fast approaching when the lack of this capability will become a world problem. It is against this background that the challenge of space exploration should ultimately be assessed.

Although there is little hope of space exploration providing any short-term solution to the problems of population pressure, there is a real possibility of Earth becoming a parent planet with colonies of human beings flourishing on other planets in the solar system and elsewhere. Such developments will not take place for many decades or even centuries, as there are several generations of exploration and planetary engineering to be fulfilled before any such exodus could become technically feasible, and by that time mankind must have controlled the population pressure or Industrial Civilisation will have been destroyed by it. More immediately, there is a realistic hope that it will be practicable to exploit minerals on the moon and the inner planets (Mercury, Venus, Mars) which are becoming rare on Earth. The technologies necessary to achieve this objective could be developed within a few decades, being an extension of those which have been established in the current space programmes, and the possibilities of seeking vital minerals even further afield are tantalising. Even more important than these physical aspects of expansion into extra-terrestrial space, however, are the psychic benefits. Throughout the millennia of his existence on planet Earth, *homo sapiens* has shown enormous resourcefulness and adaptability in pitting his intelligence against seemingly insoluble problems, to harness the fire of the gods, to make two blades of grass grow where only one grew before, to create wealth by his skill and diligence. As we approach the end of the twentieth century, mankind finds that he has tackled most of the challenges of his natural terrestrial environment. There are still some mountains to be climbed 'because they are there', some jungles to be tamed, some deserts to be brought to fruition. But beyond these man requires a challenge to stimulate his spirit of adventure and creative genius. The arrival of the Space Age has thus come at a most appropriate moment to provide mankind with precisely the sort of spiritual challenge which he needs to give him an endless series of goals in the aeons which lie ahead of him.

It will be a little while yet before mankind is ready to undertake the colonisation of the universe. But the possibility of such a cosmic mission is within his grasp. As with other aspects of man's future, such as the prospect of a stable world community based on principles of brotherhood and democracy, the Utopia of an ideal society need no longer be regarded as remote and impractical. Virtually all that is necessary to achieve it is to agree on our objectives and to assert our human wills in achieving them. The fact that such agreement and common action require a common purpose which has so far eluded mankind is discouraging. Yet the remedy for this tragic failure is within man's power, and if he fails to seize this manifest destiny he will have only himself to blame. Should he succeed in taking this epochal opportunity, however, the universe will lie open to him in the vast periods of time stretching out ahead. Whether or not pioneers from planet Earth encapsulated in star-ships of as yet incomprehensible size and power and venturing on the vast abyss of interstellar space, will encounter other intelligent races on their travels cannot yet be resolved. What is certain, however, is that to have reached the level of communal maturity at which such an encounter becomes possible (other than on the initiative of the alien race), mankind must have perfected the social techniques ensuring his own survival. The goals by which man must work out his own salvation in the present century take him in the same direction as those which will set his steps on the path to the stars.

The perspectives of time thus provide close bonds between past, present, and future. History, as we have seen, is an ancient study as man has always been curious about his past. But his ability to think historically has been constricted by the limited time-scale which blinkered speculation about historical processes, until the intellectual revolution of the nineteenth century opened up the past just as it opened up the future. With this new perspective we have been able to approach the vast repository which comprises man's experience of his past and seek such guidance as we can from it in framing answers to the pressing problems of the present and the more speculative projections of the distant future. Our conclusions, although only sketched in outline, are firm enough to support the contention that there is a useful function for such applied history. Not only has it been demonstrated that there are some important lessons, both general and particular, to be derived from the study of history, but also an interpretation of Industrial Civilisation has been elaborated which indicates many themes and comparisons which are highly relevant to any assessment of the prospects of this civilisation. Both the lessons and the interpretations are subject to qualification by subsequent discussion, and no body of specialists is more expert than that of professional historians in effacing the general significance of their own enquiries. But on one point, if on no other, this study leaves no reasonable ground for doubt: if Industrial Civilisation is to have any chance of solving the formidable problems which threaten to overwhelm it in the present century, it must be by the application of historical experience. In the last analysis, this is the only experience by which man can illuminate his contemporary problems and arrive at an understanding of the processes of which he is a part.

References and Further Reading

As a matter of policy, references have been kept as few as possible in this book, because it has been intended to present a comprehensive historical interpretation for a general readership so that an elaborate scholarly apparatus of footnotes would not have been appropriate. Nevertheless, it was decided to give key references, although to do so as unobstrusively as possible by combining them at the end of the main text. The general rule which has been followed in most instances has been to refer readers to easily available editions of books which provide useful elaboration of points made in the text, and with this purpose in view Penguin Classics and other paperback editions have been especially valuable. But with the whole library of works on Western Civilisation and Industrial Civilisation to choose from there has been a serious embarrassment of riches, and it is not possible to satisfy all readers with the scanty selection made here.

(Unless otherwise stated London is the place of publication.)

1. Introduction

References

1. H. Butterfield, *The Whig Interpretation of History* (Bell 1931, recently republished as a Pelican Book, 1973).
2. K. Popper, *The Poverty of Historicism*, 2nd ed. (Routledge, 1957), p. 3.
3. H. Perkin, 'Social History', in H. P. R. Finberg (ed.), *Approaches to History* (Routledge, 1962), pp. 51–82.

Further Reading

Historians are fond of discussing the uses and abuses of history, and there are some excellent books on the subject. R. G. Collingwood, *The Idea of History*, first published by the Clarendon Press, Oxford, in 1946, remains a classic, although not easy reading. See also: E. H. Carr, *What is History?* (London: Macmillan, 1961); J. H. Plumb, *The Death of the Past* (Macmillan, 1969); G. R. Elton, *The Practice of History* (Fontana, 1969); and A. Marwick, *The Nature of History* (London: Macmillan, 1970) for a useful summary of the discussion. G. Barraclough, *An Introduction to Contemporary History* (Pelican, 1967), is an interesting if provocative point of view; and W. H. Walsh, *Introduction to Philosophy of History* (Hutchinson, 1950) is a good survey of this difficult aspect of the subject. Sidney Pollard, *The Idea of Progress* (C. A. Watts, 1968, Pelican, 1971), deals with a theme which is very relevant to the argument of this book.

2. Society and Civilisation

References

1. V. Gordon Childe, *What Happened in History*, first published by Penguin in 1942 but subsequently reissued many times and still one of the most stimulating introductions to the subject.

2. Jane Jacobs, *The Economy of Cities* (USA 1969, Cape 1970, Pelican ed., 1972), especially chapter 1.

3. Arnold Toynbee, *A Study of History*. The first volume of this twelve-volume work was published in 1934, and the last in 1961. Useful 'Abridgements' have been published by D. C. Somervell, and in 1972 Dr Toynbee himself published a richly illustrated one-volume edition (Oxford University Press and Thames & Hudson) with the assistance of Miss Jane Caplan. Dr Toynbee's views have developed quite significantly over the years, and I am here adopting his more optimistic conclusions. His calculation of the number of civilisations has grown from 21 to 31, and I adopt a median position as represented in the excellent summary and presentation of the Toynbee thesis in Edward J. Myers, *Education in the Perspective of History* (Longman, 1963).

Further Reading

Archaeological studies, from which most of our knowledge of pre-civilised societies and early civilisations has been derived, have made great progress in recent decades with the development of new techniques such as carbon-dating, pollen analysis, and aerial photography. A useful introduction to the subject is Stuart Piggott, *Approach to Archaeology* (Pelican, 1966). See also: Glyn Daniels, *The First Civilisations* (Thames & Hudson, 1968), and J. G. D. Clark, *Prehistoric Europe – The Economic Basis* (Methuen 1952) and Jacquetta Hawkes, *The First Great Civilizations* (Hutchinson, 1973; Pelican 1977). A background to the intricate and, to most western readers, remote developments of Chinese civilisation will be found in John Hay, *Ancient China* (Bodley Head, 1973).

3. The City and the Individual

References

1. K. Popper, *The Open Society and its Enemies*, 2 vols (Routledge, 1945).
2. For a recent account of the collapse of the Western Roman Empire, see chapters 1 and 2 by Aurelio Bernari and M. I. Finley in C. M. Cipolla (ed.), *The Economic Decline of Empires* (Methuen, 1970).
3. Martin Buber, *Moses* (East and West Library, 1946), gives a moving and scholarly reconstruction of this legendary figure.

Further Reading

The riches of Hellenic civilisation have attracted historians of art, literature, architecture, and science as well as less specialised historians, and in addition to this wealth of secondary authorities there are many of the classical texts easily available in good translations. The Penguin Classics, for example, have issued Herodotus, *The Histories* and Thucydides, *The Peloponnesian War*, as well as Plato, *The Republic*, and many of the other 'Dialogues'. Amongst the secondary works, H. D. F. Kitto, *The Greeks* (Pelican, 1951), and R. H. Barrow, *The Romans* (Pelican, 1949) are particularly convenient summaries. M. I. Finley, *The Use and Abuse of History* (Chatto & Windus, 1975) brings a powerful scholarly mind to bear on some of the problems of ancient history. On the religious traditions, a perusal of the Old Testament is still a surprisingly rewarding exercise, while the New Testament contains many indications of the tension between Hebraic and Hellenic traditions (see especially the Acts of the Apostles).

4. The Rise of Western Civilisation

References

1. It has been necessary to cut some corners to deal with the complexities of feudalism here. For the outstanding scholarly treatment, however, see M. Bloch, *Feudal Society* (English ed., Routledge, 1961).

2. For a good summary of the economic and social aspects of Medieval expansion, see M. M. Postan, *The Medieval Economy and Society* (London: Weidenfeld and Nicolson, 1972).

3. The term 'middle class' is used here despite the trenchant and entertaining critique of J. H. Hexter, 'The Myth of the Middle Class in Tudor England', in *Reappraisals in History* (Longmans 1961). While it is conceded that the rise of the middle class must not be over-used as an explanatory concept, the term serves to describe a significant realignment in late medieval society and as such it is worth retaining.

4. A. P. D'Entreves provided a useful introduction to Thomist thought in *Aquinas: Selected Political Writings* (Basil Blackwell, 1948).

5. A recent assessment of the achievement of the medieval cathedral builders can be found in chapter 1 of Arnold Pacey, *The Maze of Ingenuity* (Allen Lane, 1974).

6. The outstanding study on this subject is Lynn White Jr, *Medieval Technology and Social Change* (Oxford University Press, 1962).

7. The authority on medieval universities is H. Rashdall, *Universities of Europe in the Middle Ages*, 3 vols (Oxford University Press, 1936). But for a colourful account of student life, see H.

Waddell, *Wandering Scholars* (Constable, 1927; Doubleday, N. Y., 1955), and the same authoress's evocation of the life of *Peter Abelard* (Holt, N. Y., 1947).

Further Reading

Some excellent general works have been written recently on the medieval centuries, and are available in paperback. See, for instance: Denys Hay, *The Medieval Centuries* (Methuen, University Paperbacks, 1964); Hugh Trevor Roper, *The Rise of Christian Europe* (Thames & Hudson, 1965), and John B. Morrall, *The Medieval Imprint* (Pelican, 1970). On a more particular (but central) theme, see also Christopher Brooke, *The Twelfth Century Renaissance* (Thames & Hudson, 1969). J. Gimpel, *The Medieval Machine* (Gollancz, 1976) has some lively thoughts on early European industrialisation.

5 The Mainspring of European Growth

References

1. The technological advantages of the European newcomers to the Indian Ocean are admirably represented in C. M. Cipolla, *Guns and Sails in the Early Phase of European Expansion* (Collins, 1965).

2. Mercantilism continues to be a theme much discussed by European historians. The most substantial treatment was E. F. Heckscher, *Mercantilism*, 2 vols (London: Allen & Unwin, 1935) but this is now somewhat dated. W. Minchinton (ed.) *Mercantilism* (D. C. Heath & Co, Boston US, 1969) is a useful compilation of various points of view on the subject.

3. The image of Europe being intellectually stood on its head is used in Herbert Butterfield, *The Origins of Modern Science* (Bell, 1949). This book still provides a stimulating introduction to the subject. See also A. Rupert Hall, *The Scientific Revolution* (London: Longmans, 1962) for a more technical treatment.

4. Max Weber, *The Protestant Ethic and the Spirit of Capitalism* (first published 1904–5, English edition, Allen & Unwin, 1930). Extracts from the main contributions to the scholarly controversy which has followed this seminal essay are collected in *Protestantism*

and Capitalism: The Weber Thesis and its Critics, edited by Robert W. Green in the series 'Problems in European Civilization', (D. C. Heath & Co., Boston, US, 1959).

5. Adam Smith, *An Inquiry into the Nature and causes of the Wealth of Nations*, Book II, ch. 3, 'Of the Accumulation of Capital, or of unproductive Labour'. In the edition of 1786, this quotation is on p. 13 of vol. II.

Further Reading

The important themes of 'early modern' European history incorporated in this chapter can be pursued at greater depths in standard works such as the *New Cambridge Modern History*, or in the volumes of a series such as the Longman *General History of Europe*. But the themes have been the subject of such intensive research by generations of European scholars that it is impossible to do justice to them in a brief bibliographical note. On the Renaissance, for instance, J. Burckhardt wrote the classic study in the nineteenth century *The Civilization of the Renaissance in Italy* (1878), and several of his interpretations have been substantially modified by later researchers such as Hans Baron, who established the primacy of civic humanism over the role of the princes in the emergence of the Quattrocento in Florence: *The Crisis of the Early Italian Renaissance – Civic Humanism and Republican Liberty in an Age of Classicism and Tyranny* (Princeton, N. J., US, 1955).

6. *The Promethean Revolution*

References

1. I have used the title 'The Promethean Revolution: Science, Technology and History' for an essay in A. Rupert Hall and Norman Smith (eds), *History of Technology, 1976* (Mansell, 1976). The mythological allusion was made by David S. Landes, *The Unbound Prometheus* (Cambridge University Press, 1970), and since then P. Mathias has asked 'Who unbound Prometheus?' in *Science and Society, 1600–1900*, a collection of essays edited by him (Cambridge University Press, 1972).

2. For a useful summary of the demographic factor in modern

history, see H. J. Habakkuk, *Population growth and economic development since 1750* (Leicester, 1971).

3. These words were part of Thomas Savery's patent specification of 1698 for the steam pump which he later described as 'the miner's friend'. The history of the steam engine has been reviewed recently in R. A. Buchanan and G. Watkins, *The Industrial Archaeology of the Stationary Steam Engine* (Allen Lane, 1976).

4. The discussion of the historical roots of social class can be pursued in Harold Perkin, *The Origins of Modern English Society 1780–1880* (Routledge, 1969) and E. P. Thompson, *The Making of the English Working Class* (Gollancz, 1965). See also Asa Briggs, 'The Language of "Class" in Early Nineteenth Century England' in A. Briggs and J. Saville (eds), *Essays in Labour History* (London: Macmillan, 1969).

5. Despite the 'dating' of much of the contemporary commentary, James Burnham, *The Managerial Revolution*, first published in America in 1941, Penguin 1945, is still a very penetrating insight into the theoretical and practical problems of maintaining the relevance of the Marxist critique.

6. The literature on Marxism is vast. An excellent new English edition of *Capital* volume 1 is now available in Pelican paperback, with an introduction by Ernest Mandel (Penguin, 1976). Read selectively and with discrimination, there is no better way of gaining familiarity with Marx's thought. The volume ends with a useful 'Chronology of Works by Marx and Engels', which may suggest items for further reading.

Further Reading

Industrialisation has been a subject of dominant interest to economic historians, and there is a large literature on the industrial revolution, ranging from Arnold Toynbee, *Lectures on the Industrial Revolution in England* (Rivingtons 1884; new edition David & Charles, Newton Abbott, 1969) to current exchanges in the *Economic History Review*. There is a useful collection of contributions and a bibliographical essay by the editor in R. M. Hartwell (ed.), *The Causes of the Industrial Revolution in England* (Methuen, 1967).

7. The Ascendancy of Europe

References

1. John Locke's most important political works were his two *Treatises of Civil Government* (1690) of which the second is the most relevant to this discussion. Montesquieu elaborated some of Locke's ideas in *L'esprit des lois* (1748) and helped to give them general currency in the Europe and America of the eighteenth century.

2. A precise definition of 'socialism' has become impossible, because it has come to mean such different things to different people. But C. A. R. Crosland, who said that 'socialism is about equality', made a valiant effort at giving fresh insight into its meaning in *The Future of Socialism* (Cape, 1956; revised ed., 1964).

3. The complex controversies of the English Civil Wars have been much illuminated in recent years by the work of C. Hill. See, for instance, *The World turned upside down* (Temple Smith, 1972, Penguin, 1975). The experience of the 'Levellers' and other extreme 'left-wing' groups anticipated to a remarkable degree developments in the nineteenth and twentieth centuries.

4. E. G. Wakefield expressed his views on systematic colonisation in *England and America* (1833) and *A view of the art of colonization* (1849), and they were subjected to ironical treatment by Karl Marx in the final chapter of *Capital*, vol. i (1867), ch. 33, 'The modern theory of colonization'.

5. The references here are to J. A. Hobson, *Imperialism: A study* (Constable, 1902) and to V. I. Lenin, *Imperialism, the Highest Stage of Capitalism* (1916). For a more recent treatment, see: G. Lichtheim, *Imperialism* (Praeger, USA, 1971; Pelican, 1974).

Further Reading

The themes covered in this chapter may be pursued in the vast literature of modern European history and political thought. A useful introduction is D. Thompson, *Europe since Napoleon* (Longman, 1957; Pelican 1966). N. Hampson has written a recent monograph on *The Enlightenment* (Pelican, 1968).

8. The Twentieth-century World

References

1. The fiftieth anniversary of the outbreak of hostilities occurred in 1964 and produced a rash of studies. A particularly perceptive contribution was that of A. J. P. Taylor, *The First World War: An Illustrated History* (Hamish Hamilton 1963).

2. See R. E. Schofield, *The Lunar Society of Birmingham* (Oxford 1963).

3. The terms were incorporated in the title of D. de Solla Price, *Little Science, Big Science* (Columbia University Press, USA 1963). On this and related problems, see also J. R. Ravetz, *Scientific Knowledge and its Social Problems* (Oxford University Press, 1971).

4. See W. H. G. Armytage, *A Social History of Engineering* (Faber, 1961), ch. 22, p. 251.

5. See H. & S. Rose, *Science and Society* (Allen Lane 1969; Pelican 1970), ch. 4, 'The Physicists' War', p. 58.

6. The case has been stated by J. Ellul, *The Technological Society* (1965).

7. J. K. Galbraith, *The Affluent Society* (Hamish Hamilton 1958; Pelican 1962).

8. The debate was summed up most succinctly by E. P. Thompson, *The Making of the English Working Class* (Gollancz 1963), ch. 6, 'Exploitation'.

9. K. Marx, *Das Kapital*, vol. 1 (1867). There is an excellent but bulky new edition available in paperback by Penguin, ed. E. Mandel (1976).

10. The term was coined by Thorstein Veblen, *The Theory of the Leisure Class* (Macmillan, N.Y., USA, 1912).

Further Reading

Despite all the difficulties and dangers of 'contemporary history', some excellent historical work has been done on twentieth-century themes such as the monumental study by E. H. Carr *A History of Soviet Russia*, 4 vols (Macmillan, 1950–71; Penguin, 1966–76), and the wars of the century have attracted a plethora of attention, largely journalistic but including some good scholarship. For a thought-provoking general introduction, see G. Barraclough, *An Introduction to Contemporary History* (C. A. Watts 1964; Pelican 1967).

9. The Lessons of History

References

1. For further details on Marx, see Chapter 6, note 6, and on Toynbee see Chapter 2, note 3. The other reference is Oswald Spengler, *The Decline of the West*, the first part of which was originally published in German in 1918. It was translated into English in the 1920s and there is a useful one-volume edition translated by C. F. Atkinson and published by Allen & Unwin Ltd, which has passed through several impressions.

Further Reading

As this chapter seeks to apply to the development of Industrial Civilisation some of the historical analysis discussed in the Introduction, the general references given for Chapter 1 are relevant here also.

10. The Prospects of Industrial Civilisation

References

1. S. H. Meadows et al, *The Limits to Growth* (University Books N.Y., USA, 1972; Earth Island Ltd 1972) is the best known publication of the Club of Rome. The computer projections on which this study was based have been subjected to pertinent criticism – see, for instance, H. S. D. Cole et al, *Thinking about the Future – A Critique of Limits to Growth* (Chatto & Windus for Sussex University Press, 1973).

2. The concept of stable equilibrium is an attempt to take into account the powerful arguments advanced by the ecologists in recent years. Rachel Carson, *Silent Spring* (Hamish Hamilton, 1963) was a pioneer in calling attention to environmental pollution, and was the first person to make the American and British public aware of the

serious consequences of using insecticides indiscriminately. See also Barbara Ward and René Dubos, *Only One Earth: the care and maintenance of a small planet* (Andre Deutsch and Pelican, 1972), and Richard G. Wilkinson, *Poverty and Progress* (Methuen 1973). The latter is a particularly forceful exposition of the dangers of disturbing ecological equilibrium.

3. Thomas More's *Utopia* was written in Latin and first published in 1516. There is a good edition available in Penguin Classics, ed. Paul Turner (1965). It is significant that More coined the word 'Utopia' as a rather ironical pun, capable of meaning either 'no place' or 'the good place'.

4. For a recent treatment of secularisation in a historical context, see Owen Chadwick, *The Secularization of the European Mind in the Nineteenth Century* (Cambridge 1975).

5. Alvin Toffler, *Future Shock* (1970 and Pan Books, 1975).

6. The course of this particularly important aspect of the European intellectual revolution has been admirably surveyed by Stephen Toulmin and June Goodfield, *The Discovery of Time* (Hutchinson 1965; Pelican 1967). This has been available in Pelican, as has also Charles Darwin, *The Origin of Species* (1859), which is delightfully easy to read.

7. Apart from the well-known classics of science fiction – Jules Verne, H. G. Wells, and so on – which are still eminently readable, many less familiar works are worth careful consideration. In particular, Olaf Stapledon, *Last and First Men* (1930; Penguin 1963) is a projection of extraordinary imaginative power, and amongst more recent authors Arthur C. Clarke possesses an outstanding capacity for plausible inventiveness. Although it is not strictly science fiction, Clarke's *Profiles of the Future* (Gollancz, 1962; Pan Books 1964) is a brilliant evocation of the imaginative possibilities (and impossibilities) before mankind.

'Futurology' has aspirations of becoming a science in its own right, and although the treatment of the future prospects of our civilisation in this chapter does not claim to belong to this genre, there is a considerable literature readily available which is relevant to several aspects of the discussion here.

INDEX

DATE DUE

GAYLORD			PRINTED IN U.S.A.